# The Gospel
# of Philip

Books in the
## SkyLight Illuminations Series

# The Gospel of Philip

Annotated & Explained

Translation and Annotation by
Andrew Phillip Smith

Foreword by Stevan Davies

*Walking Together, Finding the Way*
SKYLIGHT PATHS®
PUBLISHING
Woodstock, Vermont

*The Gospel of Philip:*
*Annotated & Explained*

2005 First Printing
Translation, annotation, and introductory material © 2005 by Andrew Phillip Smith
Foreword © 2005 by Stevan Davies

**Library of Congress Cataloging-in-Publication Data**
Smith, Andrew Phillip, 1966–
The Gospel of Philip annotated and explained / translation and annotation by Andrew
Phillip Smith ; foreword by Stevan Davies.
p. cm. — (Skylight illuminations series)
Includes bibliographical references.
ISBN 1-59473-111-X (pbk.)
1. Gospel of Philip (Coptic Gospel)—Criticism, interpretation, etc. I. Gospel of
Philip (Coptic Gospel). English. II. Title. III. Series: SkyLight illuminations.
BS2860.P67S65 2005
229'.8—dc22                                                            2005015517
10  9  8  7  6  5  4  3  2  1

Manufactured in the United States of America
Cover Design: Walter C. Bumford III, Stockton, Massachusetts
Cover Art: courtesy of thebiblerevival.com

SkyLight Paths Publishing is creating a place where people of different spiritual
traditions come together for challenge and inspiration, a place where we can
help each other understand the mystery that lies at the heart of our existence.

SkyLight Paths sees both believers and seekers as a community that increasingly transcends traditional boundaries of religion and denomination—people
wanting to learn from each other, *walking together, finding the way*.

SkyLight Paths, "Walking Together, Finding the Way" and colophon are trademarks of
LongHill Partners, Inc., registered in the U.S. Patent and Trademark Office.

*Walking Together, Finding the Way*
Published by SkyLight Paths Publishing
A Division of LongHill Partners, Inc.
Sunset Farm Offices, Route 4, P.O. Box 237
Woodstock, VT 05091
Tel: (802) 457-4000    Fax: (802) 457-4004
www.skylightpaths.com

For Tessa Finn and Dylan Smith

# Contents ☐

# Foreword ☐

**Stevan Davies**

From the time of the Gospel of Thomas, where we hear that "the Kingdom of the Father is already spread out on the earth, and people aren't aware of it" (saying 113), continuing on into the world of Sufi Islam and other mysticisms today, spiritual people have sought to see underneath and beyond appearances, to find the Divine hidden here. The Gospel of Philip is in this tradition, one where "the world has become the aeon and the aeon is fullness for him ... hidden in a perfect day and a holy light" (section 107).

The author of the Gospel of Philip is fascinated by the occult, by hiddenness, and by the secrets that lie behind and beneath appearances. The Gospel of Philip finds hidden meaning in the world, in the aeon beyond and within the world, and in the sayings of Jesus and the sacramental language of the Gnostic Christian church. Many of the passages in this text are about words, the secret meanings of words, the allegorical significance of parables, and the power of divine names. The author seeks to show the hidden meaning behind what Hinduism calls the names and forms. In section 68 we hear of three physical locations for sacrifice in Jerusalem and how each one allegorically represents an aspect of the Christian faith. In section 80, the only one to mention the apostle Philip, that apostle tells a short tale that is immediately allegorized to explain its secret meaning. We hear in section 105 that while at present we have the things of this creation, behind those appearances "the mysteries of truth are revealed in type and image." We read in section 59 that "truth did not come into the world naked, but came in types and images," an idea that can be traced to the great philosopher Plato. This Gospel is not just a set of doctrinal truths laid out on the page; it is a set of spiritual exercises helping to train readers to take types and images and find truth within them.

In this Gospel the world is a text (a very postmodern idea from this second-century document), and the duty of the Christian is to read through its allegories to the truth it hides. The Gospel of Philip shows how to interpret the world textually, advocating a hermeneutic approach to spirituality and to reality itself. It argues that there are names and realities behind those names, and that the world itself is an allegory, a set of manifest appearances that we can interpret like a text to reveal deeper and more complex meanings. We must go beyond the types and images to the ultimate source that dwells in them now.

Of all the aspects of the world, sexuality is the one to which most people, including the author of the Gospel of Philip, give most of their attention. The Christianity that became the standard church tended to regard sexuality as akin to the demonic. But the Gnostic Christianity of the Gospel of Philip finds sexuality to be akin to the Divine. We read about a sacramental sexual union between the divine and human in a bridal chamber understood to be the celestial realm. We are told that "everyone who enters the bridal chamber will kindle the light.... If anyone becomes a son of the bridal chamber, he will receive the light" (section 107).

Human mythic history is embedded in a sexual metaphor. Sections 70–71 discuss how it was that Adam (soul) has a companion, Eve (spirit), with whom he was united. But Eve separated from Adam and death came into being. Christ came to "correct the separation that has existed from the beginning, by uniting the two together" in the bridal chamber; there spirit unites with the spirit, the Word with the Word, and so forth. Those who are united sexually in the bridal chamber of the higher reality are able to become human, spirit, Word, and light. "If you become one of those from above, it is those from above who will rest on you" (section 96).

The ritual of the bridal chamber seems to empower a person to give birth to a higher Self, to become what is envisioned in the light of the rite. According to one of the most striking passages in the Gospel of Philip, "In the world of truth, if you see anything of that place you become one with what is there. You saw the spirit and you became the spirit; you saw the Christ you became the Christ.... In that other place you do see yourself—and you shall become what you see" (section 38). This is powerful writing meant to provide a path toward understanding, to guide toward experience.

The Secret Book of John, another Nag Hammadi text, conveys the fundamental Gnostic myth of creation by telling the story of humankind's imprisonment in a dark world apart from the true God. The Gospel of Philip is based on this myth and occasionally refers to important aspects of it. For example, we hear about attempts by the rulers of this world to deceive humankind, and of the holy spirit's turning the tables on those rulers. Through her deception, the holy spirit "accomplished everything through them, as she wished" (section 12). The great difference between the Secret Book of John and the Gospel of Philip is that while the former does eventually end on a positive note, showing humanity saved through the power of God's providence, it is mainly a rather gloomy account of the fall and imprisonment of God's wisdom in this lower place. The Gospel of Philip, in contrast, is filled with rejoicing and happiness at the salvation through Christ that already has taken place.

We read of the wonders of the rite of the bridal chamber and the gift of the holy spirit that cannot be taken away. We read of the future resurrection that depends upon our being raised already now, and how we will surely escape from this world in the future because we have been given the rites and the light that will guarantee our perseverance into the higher world. In this world we receive the truth in types and images; in the higher world we will see it face to face. The Gospel of Philip speaks of and to people who have been and who will be saved from the world; this Gospel is what the Gnostic religion of the Secret Book of John became after a generation or two of integration with Christianity.

The Gospel of Philip tells us that the truth cannot be found through words alone. Rather, words and the world are types and images pointing toward the truth. Therefore neither my comments here nor Andrew Phillip Smith's valuable, detailed discussion of the Gospel of Philip should substitute for your own decipherment or for your own engagement in getting beneath the types and images to the reality that lies behind them. Like the Gospel of Thomas and, to a degree, the Gospels of Mark and John, the Gospel of Philip is a spiritual exercise, a collection of riddles and enigmas that should enable us to move above the level of the things that are revealed in this world, to the level of the things that are hidden. Ideally, eventually, through our own effort, the perfect things will open to us. Along with the hidden things of truth, the holies of holies will be revealed, and the bridal chamber will invite us in (section 105).

# Introduction □

The Gospel of Philip is one of the most exciting of the Gnostic texts found in Nag Hammadi, Egypt, in 1945. In comparison with the Gospel of Thomas, which has generated a huge amount of scholarly and popular interest, the Gospel of Philip has, until recently, received relatively little recognition. The Gospel of Thomas is set apart from all of the other texts in the Nag Hammadi library by its strong claim to be as old as the gospels in the New Testament. Many people have read or at least have some familiarity with the New Testament, and the roots of Christianity in the first century and the figure of Jesus fascinate people in a way that the development of Christianity in the second century does not.

The Gospel of Philip cannot claim a first-century date. It belongs to the same second- and third-century period as most of the Gnostic Nag Hammadi texts, but its contents are a good deal more accessible than many of them. Much of its imagery is also found in the New Testament, or in the Gospel of Thomas for that matter. It draws on the imagery of the natural world, the relationships between women, men, and family, and the ancient distinctions between lords and servants, between free people and slaves, and between pagans, Jews, and Christians. The Gospel of Philip represents a genuinely spiritual development of Christianity that uses the same language and sees itself as expressing the same truths as the teachings of Jesus and Paul.

The Gospel of Philip's major claim to fame is its mention of Mary Magdalene as "the companion of the Savior" (section 48). This has been the subject of a good deal of speculation concerning Jesus's marital status, which has culminated in the extraordinarily successful novel *The Da Vinci Code*. As many critics have pointed out, author Dan Brown's claims in the novel, though fascinating, do not hold up to historical analysis. There is no reason to consider that the Gospel of Philip's references to Mary Magdalene and Jesus are in any way historical. I am sure that the compiler of the Gospel of Philip would have considered historical enquiry to be very far from the purpose of these writings. Yet the Gospel of Philip, along with other ancient texts, does assign a positive and, in many ways, preferential role to Mary. Although it falls rather short of delineating the family tree of Jesus's descendants, or of narrating Jesus's nuptial arrangements, the Gospel of Philip has a refreshingly unembarrassed attitude to sexuality, and in Philip the coupling of the bride and bridegroom represents the culmination of spiritual development.

The hero of *The Da Vinci Code* is a professor of symbology. There is actually no such academic discipline with this name, but Dan Brown has hit the nail on the head here, since symbolism and metaphor are at the heart of the Gospel of Philip. There is scarcely a single section of the Gospel of Philip that is not based upon figurative meaning. So, despite its many inaccuracies, *The Da Vinci Code* may do a great service for the ancient works such as the Gospel of Philip. As scholar Stevan Davies wrote, "Fiction featuring unorthodox ancient texts will continue to populate best-seller lists. One hopes that this will, in turn, give rise to increased interest in the realities behind the fictions, the ancient teachings of Jesus and about Jesus that really were found in 1945 in Nag Hammadi, Egypt, after having been hidden for 1,600 years."[1]

The discovery of this ancient library is a fascinating tale in its own right. In December 1945, Mohammed Ali es-Samman, an Arab camel driver, and his brother Khalifah Ali were out looking for fertilizer and found a large earthenware jar at the bottom of the high chalk cliff of Djebel-el-Tarif. They smashed open the jar, slightly wary of what they might find, only to discover twelve books. (One of the books had another book bound into it, so the books are now numbered as being thirteen in total.)

What the Egyptians had found were twelve codices. A codex is a manuscript book, which was copied by hand before the invention of printing. These are not scrolls, which are continuous sheets rolled up rather like rolls of wallpaper and are still used, for instance, in traditional Jewish religious worship, the best example being the Torah scroll. The codices are made from papyrus cut into sheets and bound between covers. They really are the forerunner of the modern book. Many people, including Dan Brown, confuse the Dead Sea Scrolls with the Nag Hammadi finds, since the two discoveries were made within two years of each other. The Dead Sea Scrolls are, as their name suggests, scrolls that were discovered in 1947 in the region of the Dead Sea in Israel and were manufactured more than three hundred years before the Nag Hammadi codices. Unfortunately—and this is the kind of inaccuracy that does not endear Dan Brown to academic scholars—Brown writes that the Dead Sea Scrolls contain Gnostic gospels (which they do not, since these scrolls are Jewish, not Christian) and that the Nag Hammadi library is written on scrolls (which they are not, although, unlike the Dead Sea Scrolls, they do contain works that are titled gospels).

The covers of the Nag Hammadi codices are of leather with a clasp extending from the back to the front. Thus, they look rather like a modern briefcase or attaché case. The Gospel of Philip is found in Codex II, which also contains the Gospel of Thomas—Philip actually follows immediately after Thomas, starting two-thirds down the final page of Thomas. Other notable works in this most important codex of the Nag Hammadi library include the Exegesis of the Soul, which interprets the Bible and Homer in terms of the ancient and Platonic idea of the soul that has fallen from its previously divine state and must make its way back to God; the Book of Thomas the Contender, which claims to be written by a Matthaias who recorded the teaching given by Jesus to Thomas; and a version of the Secret Book or Apocryphon of John, which is probably the most important text of classical Gnosticism. All of the Nag Hammadi codices are written in Coptic, which is the final stage of the ancient Egyptian language, written in Greek letters instead of hieroglyphs, with a few extra letters to represent sounds that are lacking in the Greek language and with an extensive vocabulary of loanwords from Greek. As far as we know, Greek was the original language of every text in the collection.

After their discovery, the volumes eventually made their way into the hands of scholars, though their route was not very straightforward. Their journey was complicated when the brothers who had found the manuscripts took revenge on the man who had killed their father. They murdered their father's murderer and had to go into hiding. They left the books with a Coptic priest whose brother, having some inkling of their potential value, sold a volume to an antiques dealer. Through a variety of sales, attempted sales, and peregrinations from country to country, the entire collection was ultimately preserved at the Cairo Museum.

The original manuscripts had already partly disintegrated due to their extreme age and the lack of care that followed their discovery, and so we have holes in the pages or we lack parts of the pages where the papyrus has crumbled away. Where the missing material cannot be reconstructed, these lacunae (or gaps in the manuscript) are indicated by ellipses in the text. Other lacunae are not indicated in this translation because scholars have come to a reasonable consensus about which words can be used to fill the gaps.

The Gospel of Philip, rather like the Gospel of Thomas, presents a series of discourses, parables, and sayings that often have much in common with the New Testament. Certainly there are a few references to specifically Gnostic terms that might seem meaningless out of context, especially when they are often translated by reproducing their Greek names instead of rendering them into English. Terms like *Echmoth* (Syriac for wisdom), *pleroma* (fullness), *Sophia* (wisdom), and *aeon* (the realm of eternity) occur often enough to confirm that the Gospel of Philip is indeed Gnostic, but not enough to make it as initially impenetrable and off-putting as some of the Nag Hammadi texts.

The mass of interesting material that we find spread out through this text may draw us away from a fundamental question: What is the Gospel of Philip? Why is it called a gospel? It isn't a gospel in the sense of the four canonical gospels in the New Testament, which tell stories, however symbolic or miraculous, of the life and teachings of Jesus. The Gospel of Thomas isn't a gospel in that sense either, yet it claims to be "the esoteric sayings of the living Jesus" and is clearly a collection of sayings attributed to Jesus. Most scholars nowadays are happy to classify the Gospel of Thomas as a gospel, but the Gospel of Philip hardly ever makes its way into collections of Christian gospels. It is only a gospel by virtue of its title.

The Gospel of Philip is actually an anthology of material written by Valentinians, the most subtle and appealing of early Christian movements. Once we see the Gospel of Philip as an anthology, excerpted from a group of related writings, we can understand why it jumps around from one theme to another, repeating images and subjects without warning, containing different and often contradictory twists in its approaches. At first it may seem disappointing to learn that this is an anthology, as if this format might lessen the importance of the text, or make its authenticity questionable. But this actually makes the text richer. As well as the point of view of the compiler, we have material from a variety of sources, possibly including the Gospel of Thomas.

## Valentinus's Influential Gnosticism

Some of the terms in the Gospel of Philip show that it is Gnostic. We might expect that the simple fact that the Gospel of Philip was found at Nag Hammadi with other Gnostic texts should indicate its Gnosticism, but the Nag Hammadi codices also contain a fragment of Plato's Republic, the Sentences of Sextus, which is neither Christian nor Gnostic nor Jewish, Hermetic material such as Poimandres, and the Gospel of Thomas, which lacks Gnostic technical terms and perhaps has more in common with Jewish Wisdom literature.

Philosophically, the term *Gnostic* can be used to describe a great variety of material, ranging from the prophetic books of William Blake to the premises behind the movie *The Matrix*. But historically it is used to describe the second- and third-century Christian groups that were criticized by church fathers such as Irenaeus, Tertullian, and Hippolytus. The writings of these church fathers are consistently negative, in contrast to the creative expression of Gnostic writers. But the form of Christianity championed by the church fathers won the battle for Christianity, and their writings survived, while Gnostic writings did not. Still, even among educated Christians, few have read the tedious and self-justifying writings of the second- and third-century fathers. By a quirk of fate, they are studied today primarily for the information that they give us concerning Gnosticism, and many more people now read Gnostic texts than have ever read the church fathers.

There were many varieties of Gnostic groups, and few of them even seem to have referred to themselves as Gnostics. We might look at the term *New Age* by way of comparison. Marketing aside, many people don't wish New Age to be applied to them, nor do many modern spiritual groups wish to be lumped in with other New Age groups. New Age can even be used as a term of abuse, as Gnostic certainly was. Gnosticism is a complex of communities and ideas, and the scholar Michael Williams has shown that it is very difficult to identify any common set of beliefs or characteristics that could include all of the groups and writings labeled as Gnostic.[2] Yet it remains a useful, if imprecise, category.

Luckily, we can apply a more specific name to the movement that produced the Gospel of Philip: Valentinianism. This movement takes its name from its founder, Valentinus, one of the most brilliant Gnostics. Valentinus was born on the Egyptian coast around the beginning of the second century, was educated in Alexandria, and moved to Rome halfway through the same century, during the reign of Antoninus Pius. Valentinus was in Rome at around the same time as the Christian apologist Justin Martyr. According to a tradition preserved by the heresy-hunting church father Hippolytus, Valentinus said that the Word or the *Logos* appeared to him as a newborn child. This revelation—which I suspect is more a metaphorical description of a spiritual experience than a vision, per se—prompted Valentinus to begin teaching his spiritual understanding to others. Valentinus and his followers were in many ways less radical than other Gnostics and more balanced in their approach. For the most part, their interpretations of the Hebrew Bible were not hostile to Jewish culture and traditional interpretations of the Hebrew Bible in the way that many Gnostic interpretations were. Valentinians mingled with members of the proto-orthodox church and kept many or most of the external rites and practices of Christianity. Their tendency to take part in the conventional forms of Christian worship while seeing a deeper spiritual significance in the rites led to them being called "wolves in sheep's clothing." Valentinus himself apparently hoped to become a bishop in due course and clearly hoped to influence Christianity from within, but he failed in this regard, and he was never elected as a bishop.

Most of what we know about Valentinianism comes from its critics, who are so hostile to it that we should take everything they write with a pinch of salt. For instance, Valentinus's student Marcus was accused by the church father Irenaeus of seducing his female followers, but on a closer reading this turns out not to be a sexual seduction but a doctrinal seduction.

According to Clement of Alexandria, the third-century church father who had some sympathy for and affinities with Gnosticism, Valentinus was taught by a certain Theudas, who had been taught by Paul himself. Thus, the Valentinians could make the same claim to apostolic succession as could the proto-orthodox Christians. Even if Paul had never met the earthly Jesus, he had a direct connection to the risen Christ. And even if the proto-orthodox tried to discount that, Paul had still received approval from Peter, John, and James, "the brother of the Lord."

One of the most accessible and beautiful of the Nag Hammadi writings, the Gospel of Truth, is tentatively ascribed to Valentinus, along with some poetic fragments that can be extracted from the heresiologists. One of the Valentinians' most notable characteristics was the way in which they read scripture. The Valentinians interpreted the Bible allegorically and spiritually. We shall see that there is good evidence that this kind of interpretation goes back to the earliest Christianity.

## Philip the Apostle

The Gospel of Philip is, of course, named not after Valentinus but after Philip. Who is this Philip, its purported author? As with many, if not most, of the writings that belong to early Christianity, the Gospel of Philip has no likely connection to the figure after whom it is named. Philip is mentioned only once, in section 80, and this is likely to be the entire extent of the association between Philip the apostle and the Gospel of Philip. Thus, the Gospel of Philip is an example of pseudoepigrapha, or "false writing." This was a common-enough practice in early Christianity and in the ancient world in general. Many scholars would maintain that we don't know the true name of the author of any of the gospels, including those in the New Testament. In this book, I follow the rather odd convention of scholarship in referring to the author or compiler of the Gospel of Philip as "Philip," even though no serious scholar thinks that this was the author's name.

Philip the apostle appears in the list of the twelve disciples in Mark, Matthew, and Luke, but those synoptic gospels say no more of him. It is only in the Gospel of John that he receives specific mention. According to John, Philip was from Bethsaida, as were the brothers Andrew and Peter. Andrew and an unnamed man were disciples of John the Baptist, and they met Jesus and began to follow him. Jesus then found Philip and also told him to "follow me." Philip in turn recruited Nathaniel. Before Jesus feeds the crowd, in John 6, Philip points out somewhat practically that even two hundred denarii would not buy enough bread to feed the multitude assembled there.

Philip is a Greek name that became popular because of Alexander the Great's father, Philip of Macedon. There was a fair amount of Hellenization in all areas of the Near East, including Galilee and Judea, and there was no particular contradiction in a Galilean having a Greek name. In an odd sequence in John 2, some Greeks approach Philip in Jerusalem and request that they see Jesus. When Philip and Andrew (which is also a Greek name) relay this to Jesus, he responds, "The hour has come for the son of man to be glorified. Very truly, I tell you, unless a grain of wheat falls into the earth and dies, it remains just a single grain; but if it dies, it bears much fruit." This is strongly reminiscent of the Greek mysteries, with their emphasis on seasonal rebirth and the symbolic ear of corn. At the Passover meal, in John's gospel, Philip demands of Jesus, "Lord, show us the father, and we will be satisfied." In the discourse that follows, Jesus promises that he will ask the father to send the Paraclete, who is the spirit of truth. The spirit is of primary importance in the Gospel of Philip, and there are many references to the Gospel of John in its passages.

Philip pops up again in the Acts of the Apostles, where he takes up a fair amount of chapter 8. He goes down to Samaria, ridding people of unclean spirits. There, he encounters Simon Magus, who is practicing magic and, in an interesting twist, converts Simon and teaches him. The irony here is that anti-Gnostic writers claimed that Simon was the founder of Gnosticism (and it is worth noting that by making this claim, the heresiologists are placing the origin of Gnosticism in the time of the apostles and, despite their antagonism toward Gnosticism, show that it goes back beyond the second century). So in Acts we have Philip converting to Christianity a man whom the church fathers reviled as a Gnostic, and yet Valentinian Gnostics could happily use Philip's name for a piece of Gnostic writing.

Another unusual episode follows from this in the Acts of the Apostles, where Philip meets an Ethiopian eunuch. Philip is directed by an angel of the Lord to go on the road from Jerusalem to Gaza into the desert. The angel directs Philip to enter the chariot of the eunuch, who is in the service of Queen Candace of Ethiopia. The eunuch happens to be reading from Isaiah, as the queen appears to be a Jewish convert. Philip explains to the eunuch about Jesus and, at the eunuch's request, baptizes him. This episode is the subject of the painting on the cover of this book.

Another Nag Hammadi text named after Philip is the Letter of Peter to Philip in Codex VIII. (This tract incidentally shows that Peter was not always a bogeyman for the Gnostics.) The Letter of Peter to Philip was written around the same general time as the Gospel of Philip, but since

Philip is only named as the receiver of the letter, this text gives us little extra information concerning Philip. The late Gnostic text Pistis Sophia tells us that Philip was the scribe who took down the words of Jesus.

The Acts of Philip is one of a series of second- and third-century accounts of the lives of the apostles, which survived in various manuscripts. The Acts is very much in the tradition of ancient romances, full of magic and dangerous travels, and is not a Gnostic text. In one of the episodes Philip travels to Greece and disputes with three hundred philosophers, who in turn write to Ananias, the high priest from the gospel stories. Ananias travels from Jerusalem with five hundred men, and Philip and Ananias enter a dispute. Jesus appears in the sky; Philip performs miracles that are clearly magical and that even use magical formulas. He utters the words "Zabarthan, sabathaban, bramanouch," which is a magical spell in pidgin Hebrew. Magic was part of the common culture of the ancient Mediterranean world, but perhaps Philip's association with magic stems from his encounter with Simon Magus in the Acts of the Apostles.

According to the Acts of Philip, Philip died in Hierapolis, crucified upside down on a cross along with Bartholomew. The church historian Eusebius also preserves a tradition that Philip was buried there. Although the Acts of Philip is certainly not Valentinian, there is some relationship between the Acts of Philip and the Gospel of Philip, since a few sayings pop up in both. Probably the Acts is familiar with some of the traditions in the Gospel of Philip.

### The Question of Mary Magdalene

If one figure in the Gospel of Philip is responsible for its being more widely known than other Nag Hammadi texts, that person is Mary Magdalene. Mary occurs in two sections. In section 28 we read, "There were three Marys who walked with the Lord at all times: his mother and his sister and the Magdalene, who is called his companion. So his mother and sister and companion are called 'Mary.'" Section 48 states, "And the companion of the savior is Mary Magdalene. The Lord loved Mary more than the other disciples and kissed her often on her [mouth]. The rest of them saw him loving Mary and said to him, 'Why do you love her more than us?'"

In both of these, Mary is referred to as Jesus's companion. The Coptic word used in the original text is *koinonos,* a loanword from Greek. The range of meanings includes companion or partner, but not necessarily in a sexual sense. Mary Magdalene acquired her loose reputation when she was identified with "the woman who was a sinner" in Luke 7, and the traditional figure of Mary Magdalene is a composite creation made up of various Marys and unnamed women from the canonical gospels.

Mary probably came from the city of Magdala on the Lake of Galilee. In all four of the canonical gospels, Mary Magdalene is given a special role in finding the empty tomb or witnessing the resurrection. The original ending of the earliest gospel, the Gospel of Mark, concluded with Mary Magdalene, Mary the mother of James, and Salome in the empty tomb. Mary Magdalene also has an important role in the Nag Hammadi Dialogue of the Savior, the Gospel of Thomas, and the Gnostic Gospel of Mary. We know nothing of Jesus's marital status, and there is no real evidence either for or against the possibility that he was married. As a Jewish man in the first century it was quite likely that he was married, since this was the norm, but there was also room within the culture for him to be celibate. We also know nothing of Mary Magdalene's marital status. For all we know, she may have been single, or happily married to someone else. (See the annotations to sections 28 and 48 for more on this subject.)

### Interpreting the Gospel of Philip

Since the Gospel of Philip is not the place to go for historical information about the life of Jesus, how *should* it be interpreted? I believe that the text itself tells us how we should do this. Section 59 tells us, "Truth did not come into the world naked, but came in types and images." And section 105 says, "The mysteries of truth are revealed in type and image." That is, the contents of the Gospel of Philip are not meant to be taken literally, but metaphorically. The Gospel of Philip offers a symbolic, esoteric, and allegorical interpretation of Christian and biblical material. It piles metaphor on metaphor. Terms like *bridal chamber, light, fire, water, chrism, animals, slaves, sons,* and *rest* are repeated through the Gospel of Philip.

Why is the truth expressed indirectly? Because, according to Philip, "the world cannot receive it in any other way. There is rebirth and an image of rebirth. It is truly necessary to be born again through the image. Which image? Resurrection. The image must rise again through the image. Through the image the bridal chamber and the image must enter into the truth: this is the regeneration" (section 59). Thus, "rebirth" itself is the actual spiritual experience of rebirth; the image of rebirth is only the word *rebirth* or the metaphor of rebirth. An image is spiritual reality put into words or pictures. Much of the commentary that accompanies the translation in this book is concerned with this kind of interpretation.

Of course, the problem with allegory and other interpretive methods is that they can make a text say anything that the interpreter wants it to say. We cannot pretend that all allegorical interpretations of the Bible have agreed with one another. A glance at the appropriate section of any bookstore will reveal a variety of books that offer competing and incompatible interpretations of scripture. Conservative scholars particularly have argued that Gnostics are perverting the literature of the Bible by interpreting it symbolically and not literally. While we may not be able to argue in an absolutely historical way that the kind of interpretation that is central to the Gospel of Philip derives directly from Jesus, the interpretive methods of allegory, typology, symbolism, and parable are central to early Christianity. If we look, we can find examples of this sort of thing in the New Testament.

Parables, of course, are a famous aspect of the teachings of Jesus in the gospels. If Jesus was anything, he was a teller of parables, and the subtlety of the parables of Jesus is unmatched. A parable isn't necessarily allegorical itself. A parable isn't even necessarily a story. The *Oxford Companion to the Bible* offers a succinct and useful definition: "A parable is a picturesque figure of language in which an analogy refers to a similar but different reality." Some parables in the gospels are allegorized. We are told in the Gospel of Mark, for example, that the Word is the seed. But more often a parable leaves us to find an application for it. Augustine of Hippo produced a notorious interpretation of the parable of the Good Samaritan in which every element of the parable mirrors something in church doctrine; he even goes so far as to state that the apostle Paul is the innkeeper in the story. While I wouldn't dispute that a parable may have been created with a specific meaning in mind, or even that certain symbols had specific meanings that were used fairly consistently throughout early Christianity, Augustine's example really does seem to be making the parable of the Good Samaritan say something that it was never intended to say.

The very earliest parts of the New Testament are the letters of Paul, which are dated to the 40s and 50s of the first century. The canonical gospels and the Gospel of Thomas are generally dated to the last quarter of the first century. Paul gives us our earliest glimpse of Christianity and hence—though many people shrug this off—our most authentic picture of the earliest Christianity. Most people prefer to think of the gospels as giving us the most authentic picture of early Christianity, since they are concerned with the life of Jesus, but the gospels are later and more elaborate than Paul's letters. There are many references to Paul's writings in the Gospel of Philip, and some of these are noted in the commentary.

Paul uses metaphor flamboyantly. Part of the reason that he can sometimes be so confusing is that he switches between the literal and symbolic meanings of a word. As Paul says in the King James Version, "the letter killeth, the spirit giveth life." Or as the Valentinian Theodotus put it, "Paul teaches in two ways at once." For Paul, as for the Gospel of Thomas (and to some extent Philo of Alexandria, and even books in the Hebrew Bible such as Isaiah), the notion of physical circumcision (which was not then unique to Jews, as it is not now either) is eclipsed by a metaphorical spiritual circumcision (see the annotation to section 103). Death in Paul's writings, while it sometimes denotes the death of the body, is more often a reference to the spiritual death of not having Christ within oneself. Paul specifically provides allegorical interpretations of some of the stories from the Hebrew Bible. He refers to the old Adam and the new Adam, tells us that the rock that follows Moses is Christ, that the crossing of the Red Sea is a type of baptism, that Ishmael and Isaac represent Judaism and Christianity, and so on.

The Gospel of Philip quotes from Paul as much as it quotes from the canonical gospels. In recent times Paul has acquired the reputation of being the person who twisted the original intentions of Jesus and turned a spiritual teaching into an organized religion, but the Gnostics revered him as "the great apostle." Elaine Pagels devoted an entire book, *The Gnostic Paul*, to Valentinian interpretations of Paul's letters.

Beyond Paul, we find examples in the Gospel of Mark—the first of the New Testament gospels to be written—that indicate that the surface meaning of his gospel is not the most important level of meaning. Parables and proverbs are repeatedly accompanied by the injunction, "He who has ears to hear, let him hear." The twelve disciples are told, "To you it has been given to know the mystery of the kingdom of God; but to those who are outside, all things come in parables" (Mark 4:11). When the second feeding of the multitudes occurs in Mark 8, Jesus insists that the two feedings have a meaning that the disciples do not understand, a meaning that is based on number symbolism. We are so used to reading the New Testament that we see nothing significant in the repetition of imagery. This repeated imagery is somewhat clearer in the Gospel of Thomas, since it lacks the narrative elements and is less familiar to us.[3]

Among the other New Testament texts that clearly use symbol and allegory, the Epistle to the Hebrews should be mentioned, as it takes a profound look at the symbolism of the Jerusalem Temple, as does the Gospel of Philip. Also worth noting is the Revelation of John, which scholars agree is symbolic, even if there is little agreement on what the symbolism means. The Epistle of James is also a wonderful example of early Christian imagery and metaphor.

### Soul and Spirit in the Bridal Chamber

One of Philip's most striking features is the complex of material that has as its hub the concept of the bridal chamber. A bridal chamber is a bedroom, and some translations of Philip use this word. However, "bridal chamber" is used throughout this translation because it has a more mythical sound and connotation and emphasizes that the bridal chamber is where the marriage is first consummated. This is a beautiful image: the husband and wife making love within the bridal chamber.

Images of bride, bridegroom, and weddings are surprisingly persistent throughout early Christianity. Several parables in the New Testament are based around weddings, as is the famous miracle at the wedding at Cana in the Gospel of John. The imagery of the bridal chamber is intimately connected with the distinction between male and female. Sometimes these are definitely allegorized, as in II Clement 4:2, a second-century pseudepigraphic proto-orthodox epistle, where "The male is Christ, the female is the church." The imagery of husband and wife, of male and female elements that combine to form a unity, is widespread and expands to include the entire range of (hetero)sexual relationships, or at least those that were available to the ancient world. A woman can be a virgin, a daughter, a whore, a mother, a wife. A man can be a father, a son, a celibate, a seducer, a husband. A legitimate coupling is a uniting, where the two are made into one, and this coupling takes place in the bridal chamber. An improper union involves adultery or prostitution. Although the Gospel of Philip is quite open about sexuality, no one could accuse it of impropriety in these matters.

This sexual imagery demands interpretation. The notions of male and female in the Gospel of Philip do not seem to involve the Jungian sense of anima and animus, where each person has elements of the feminine and masculine within him or her, but a specifically allegorical sense, where the female represents a specific cosmic level, and the male a different level. Philo, the first-century Hellenistic Jewish philosopher, who wrote long works that interpret scripture allegorically, thought that what is female in a person is that which is concerned with the outer senses and outer experience, whereas what is male in one is what is turned, or can turn, toward God. While we can no longer agree with these notions of gender, these concepts are very helpful in deciphering other ancient texts. On a different level, a female figure can be higher than the male, as with the feminine holy spirit.

A more exact interpretation of male and female symbolism requires that we have some understanding of ancient notions of body, soul, and spirit. These three elements make up a human being. The body needs little explanation: it is the physical body and to it belongs all that is usually called carnal. Modern notions of soul and spirit, however, are considerably less distinct than were the ancient concepts. Soul and spirit are clearly different from each other, but the difference isn't one that is familiar to the modern mind. In ancient thought, spirit is a divine level and is often specifically referred to as the holy spirit. As Paul wrote, "God is a spirit." Soul is rather more complex. The soul is what is most distinctively ourselves. Everyone has a soul, and it comes from a higher level than the body, but in its present fallen state, it no longer looks inward and upward, but looks outward, toward earthly things. It is united with the body. The soul has whored with the things of this world.

In the Nag Hammadi text the Exegesis of the Soul, which appears in the same volume as the Gospel of Philip and the Gospel of Thomas, the soul, an androgynous virgin, left the father and came down into the body, where she was set about by thieves and was used by wanton men. As Plato, whose writings had a strong influence on Gnosticism, wrote, "Once the soul had wings, but the soul lost her wings." This is also the point of the story told in the beautiful Hymn of the Pearl, which is contained in the Acts of Thomas, another of the apocryphal acts of the apostles. But the soul has the capacity to unite with the bridegroom in the bridal chamber, by the grace of the father, and to be restored and regenerated. This theme of fall and return is also the story of Sophia, or Wisdom, who plays such a significant role in so many varieties of Gnostic texts, as well as in the parts of the

Hebrew Bible and Apocrypha that comprise the Wisdom tradition. In rabbinical writings, God is sometimes described as the groom, while the seeker of God (who is almost always a man in the ancient world) is the bride.

Gnosticism has often been interpreted as being a system of philosophy or cosmological myth, but what is presented in the Gospel of Philip cannot be merely a question of imagery, but must have referred to some kind of spiritual experience. As the Gospel of Philip puts it, "You saw the spirit and became the spirit; you saw the Christ, you became the Christ; you saw the father, you shall become the father" (section 38). Paul wrote, "But he who is united to the Lord becomes one spirit with him" (1 Cor. 6:16–17).

From the point of view of ancient Gnosticism, not only were all people composed of the three elements body, soul, and (potentially) spirit, but individuals could be classified according to which of the three was predominant in them. Those who were concerned only with the physical world, for whom the body and its needs and appetites were of sole importance, were called "hylics," after the Greek word *hyle,* which means "matter." Those whose identity was in the *psyche,* the soul, were known as "psychics." For Valentinians, ordinary Christians were psychics (which, though it shares the same root, has nothing to do with modern notions of psychic powers.) The soul was believed to have fallen and united with the body, but it still had the potential to rise and return to the Father, though it had not yet done so. Gnostics also thought of Jews as psychics, whereas pagans seem to have been considered hylics. This is a key to the use of the term *Jew* or *Hebrew* in the Gospel of Philip. Conventional Jews and Christians possessed many of the same scriptures and traditions as Gnostics but did not have the experience of the spirit. The third category were known as "pneumatics," from *pneuma,* which means "spirit." Pneumatics were those who had spirit, or contact with the spirit, and had thus to some extent realized their potential and were united with or had begun to return to the Father.

The imagery of male and female and their relationship to the soul and the spirit leads inexorably to the story of Adam and Eve in Genesis. Interpretation of Genesis was practiced by all of the writers in each thread of tradition mentioned above. Many of these interpretations are noted in the appropriate sections of the commentary. Paul refers explicitly to the story of Adam, to a first Adam and second Adam, and to the serpent.[4] Jewish midrash explained difficult or contradictory elements of the original text in Genesis, and a considerable body of Jewish tradition added to the sparse originals. The Gospel of Thomas uses "imagery from the first couple of chapters of the book of Genesis. The state to which we must aspire is the state from which we have fallen. It is light, it is the spirit, it is the beginning. Just as Jesus says that life is movement and rest [Gospel of Thomas 50], so the spirit moves across the face of the waters on the third day, and God finds rest from work on the Sabbath, the seventh day in Genesis."[5]

The more revolutionary Gnostic groups flipped the account in Genesis on its head and held that the serpent, often called Samael or Yaldabaoth, was the demiurge, the jealous God of this world. Some elements of this radical tradition of reinterpreting Genesis show up in Philip, but for the most part Philip's interpretation of Genesis, which is quite extensive, has more in common with that of Paul or the Gospel of Thomas or Philo than with the revolutionary interpretations of the Apocryphon of John.

## Mystery and Meaning in Sacraments

Not everything in the Gospel of Philip is absolutely metaphorical. Even pneumatics lead earthly lives, eat and drink (although Valentinus claimed, no doubt metaphorically, that Jesus did not defecate), take part in the activities of their cultures, and engage in Valentinian practices. The church fathers sometimes give us specific details of Valentinian practices, though they are often seen through the distorting lens of a jealous orthodoxy.

Many scholars have been particularly fascinated by the references to sacraments in the Gospel of Philip. A sacrament is a specific rite in Christianity. The Latin *sacramentum* was used in the vulgate translation of the Greek New Testament to translate the Greek *mysterion,* which occurs in its Coptic form in Philip and is translated here as "mystery." Philip in section 60 tells us that "the Lord did everything in a mystery: a baptism and a chrism and a eucharist and a redemption and a holy bridal chamber."

The rites of baptism and the Eucharist, the taking of bread and wine, have inarguably been part of Christianity at least since the time of Paul, and they owe their rationale to events that are said to have happened in Jesus's lifetime. Chrism, redemption, and the bridal chamber discussed above may also have been sacramental rites. Exactly what ritual of redemption or ransom the Gospel of Philip might refer to, no one really knows, but a chrism is an anointing with oil. Irenaeus, who is always suspect in these matters, wrote that Marcosians, who were a branch of Valentinians who followed Valentinus's student Marcus, pour a mixture of oil and water "and want this to be the redemption." It is more likely that oil and water symbolize redemption in some way, though any connection with the notion of having one's debts paid, or being bought back from captivity, are unclear.

Whether or not the Gospel of Philip has in mind actual rites for each of the five sacraments, Valentinians undoubtedly practiced some of the same rituals as the Christians, who Valentinians referred to as psychics, or merely of the soul. Presumably—and there is ample evidence for this in the Gospel of Philip—Valentinians saw in these rituals hidden meanings and a relevance to the human situation, where others saw only conventional ritual.

Irenaeus tells us of a Valentinian initiation ritual conducted by the Valentinian Marcus. In his typically hostile way, he writes of a poor woman being made hysterical by the rite and presents it as a clever conjuring trick by which a larger cup is filled with wine by a smaller cup so that the larger cup overflows.[6] Irenaeus seems to think that this should terrify any poor neophyte who undergoes the initiation. But put yourself in the position of the initiate. Simply being in the role of an initiate during such an important ceremony would give you a heightened sense of awareness. As, against all expectations, the leader of the ritual continues to pour when the cup is already full, and the red wine flows out over the lip of the cup and onto the floor, you would be vividly aware of the present moment. As someone who has seen a Fourth Way teacher spontaneously overfill a glass of wine at a formal dinner, the table set with silver flatware, fine linen tablecloth and napkins, and beautiful flower arrangements, I can testify to its efficacy. The creation of a heightened sense of being aware of the present moment is at the foundation of all genuine spiritual teaching.

The Gospel of Philip tells us repeatedly that names are not reality, but are only pointers to reality that can be misused or misinterpreted, just as the Zen monk told his student not to look at his finger but at what it was pointing to. The image of rebirth is not rebirth itself. To be born spiritually in a second birth brings one into a new world, a world of the spirit that is as startlingly different to the world of the body and soul as the world of air and light is to the darkness of the womb.

The Gospel of Philip offers us an insight into the spiritual interpretation of scripture that is at the foundation of Christianity. In studying it we can obtain a greater insight into ancient Gnosticism and the New Testament. But above everything the Gospel of Philip wishes that the reader should develop the higher levels of consciousness to which it refers: "You saw the spirit and became the spirit."

## Acknowledgments

I would like to thank Stevan Davies for putting me in touch with Skylight Paths.

# A Note on the Translation □

The translation is based on the critical Coptic text established by Bentley Layton. I have drawn considerably, though cautiously, on Paterson Brown's interlinear translation from Walter Till's earlier edition of the text. I have mainly used the translations of Bentley Layton, Wesley Isenberg, and H. M. Schenke and R. McL. Wilson, but I have also consulted the David Cartlidge and David Dungan translation, Wilson's earlier translation, Jean-Yves LeLoup's interpretive translation, and Willis Barnstone's felicitous reworking of Isenberg's translation. I have adopted Bentley Layton's division of the text into sections, but it should always be borne in mind that these divisions are artificial and are not in the original Coptic text; there is actually no standard way of referring to the text apart from page and line numbers. Schenke, for instance, has adopted a system of numbering that is equally influential. In some cases I have further divided sections into subsections, purely for ease of reference. Since the components of the Gospel of Philip are not really sayings, I refer to them neutrally as sections.

The Gospel of Philip has many lacunae—gaps in the text—that are mostly due to the deterioration of the manuscript. Where these can be filled with reasonable certainty, or where there would be no controversy in filling them, I have filled in the missing material without comment. When the lacuna is too extensive, or where it cannot be reliably filled, I have indicated it using the ellipsis enclosed in brackets. Isenberg's translation in Codex II by Layton indicates all lacunae for those interested in further investigating this.

This is not a gender-neutral translation. Coptic has no neuter gender, and so every noun and pronoun is grammatically either male or female.

Symbolic divisions between male and female are important in the text, where, for example, the holy spirit is female. I do try to render "man" neutrally where possible, as mankind or humanity. Where I have been unable to do this without mangling the language, I have assumed the traditional masculine. However, I am certain that the Gospel of Philip makes no spiritual evaluation on the basis of gender.

Even though the canon of the New Testament was not firmly established by the time that the Gospel of Philip was written, the writings now known to Christians as the New Testament were widely known, and the Gospel of Philip implicitly refers to many of them. In this book, the accurate and unprejudiced term "Hebrew Bible" will be used instead of "Old Testament." Since no accurate alternative exists for "New Testament," I refer to the collection by its traditional Christian name.

Although I have capitalized God, Wisdom, and Word (Logos), terms like father, son, and holy spirit are not capitalized in this text. Philip tells us that terms like this give us the wrong ideas, which are conventional religious ideas. Not capitalizing these terms is a small way of removing our usual associations from these words. On the other hand, I have rendered technical terms like "son of man" literally, rather than using "child of the human being" or the like. Philip is interpreting scripture, and any attempt to render these terms in an untraditional way prevents us from making connections between Philip's interpretations and the New Testament texts.

To find references for quotations in the annotations, please see the Notes at the end of this book, where citations are indicated by annotation number.

# The Gospel
## of Philip

**1** The Gospel of Philip begins abruptly. Unlike many of the Nag Hammadi texts, it has no incipit (introduction) such as the Gospel of Thomas's "These are the esoteric sayings of the living Jesus" and no framing device such as the Apocryphon of James has, in which a supposed letter from James the brother of Jesus introduces the text. We are thrown in at the deep end with no explanation. These first statements in the Gospel of Philip don't provide us with any particular foundation for understanding Philip, and we could probably read the sections of the Gospel of Philip in any order. This is a confirmation that we are dealing with an anthology. The keys to interpreting the Gospel of Philip are found later in the text, for example in sections 7, 59, and 105.

**2** A proselyte is a convert to the Jewish religion, someone who is not born Jewish, and is not ethnically Jewish, but who is adopted into the Jewish religion and keeps Jewish practices including, for males, circumcision. The distinction here seems to be between someone who is born to something and someone who obtains it after birth, and also between those who have something and can give it to others, and those who have simply obtained something for themselves. The point is perhaps that of different levels of initiation. The Coptic word here means "Hebrew," not "Jew."

Later on, in section 27b, the Gospel of Philip gives us a parallel to this: The father creates a son, yet it is not possible for him who is begotten to beget others—instead, the son begets brothers, not sons.

**3** The second part of this first section is unfortunately fragmentary. Damage to the manuscript is fairly extensive in places, and some sections of the text cannot be translated, simply because they no longer exist. The first page of the Gospel of Philip is damaged at the bottom, and the second page at the top. However, the second part of this statement seems to parallel and explain the first.

*(continued on page 4)*

# ☐ The Gospel of Philip

1 A Hebrew makes a Hebrew, who is called a proselyte.[1] Yet a proselyte cannot make another proselyte.[2]

Some exist just as they [...][3] and make others like themselves, while others simply exist.

Does the compiler of the Gospel of Philip think of himself as a Jewish Christian? During the second century, a number of Christian groups, such as Ebionites and Nazoreans, continued to consider themselves to be Jews as well as Christians. They were ethnically Jewish and observed aspects of Jewish law. The rest of the Gospel of Philip doesn't suggest much to support this view. Philip seems to view Jews and non-Gnostic Christians in much the same way, as people who have not yet developed the spirit within them, but who are in a preferential position to pagans. Perhaps in this section he is not talking about Jews and Jewish converts, but about Gnostics and ordinary Christians.

**4** This is one of a series of dichotomies in Philip: in this case, one is either a son or a slave. Children and slaves are, of course, both part of a household but have very different rights and roles within that household. This is an idea that comes from Paul, in Galatians 1:7, "So through God you are no longer a slave but a son, and if a son then an heir." This echoes the previous section and gives us a parallel between a Hebrew and a proselyte and a son and a slave. This is typical of the language of the Gospel of Philip. It is not only metaphorical, but it is metaphor that is used elsewhere in early Christianity.

2a The slave only seeks to be free, he does not expect to receive the property of his lord. The son not only acts as a son, but claims his father's legacy for himself.4

**5** Now the contrast is between the living and the dead. Previously, we were told that the slave didn't inherit, but the son does, but here the dead inherit the dead, but the living inherit both the living and the dead. To be metaphorically dead, or spiritually dead, is the same as being a slave. Again, there are parallels in the writings of Paul. The Gospel of Mark tells us that God "is not God of the dead, but of the living" (12:27).

These rather elaborate statements tell us that we can move between life and death. This cannot really work on a literal level: in what way can the dead inherit the dead? The author is perhaps also thinking of Jesus's injunction to let the dead bury their dead.

**6** Here, to be dead is the same as to be a gentile. The Coptic word is based on the Greek *ethnikos,* which gives us the English word *ethnic.* An *ethnikos* is a member of the "nations," someone who isn't a Jew. In this context it also refers to someone who isn't a Christian—anyone who has believed in the truth is not a gentile.

**7** How we interpret this depends on whether we think that "Christ's coming" refers to Christ's incarnation, that is, his birth and life in our world, or that we should interpret it in a purely spiritual sense, in which Christ has come within an individual. If we take it literally, it is difficult to see how Jesus's life on earth has resulted in real cities being decorated, or in the world being created. The dead being carried out is a grisly image. It implies that the corpses have been left rotting inside houses or in the city streets. Metaphorical death runs through the Gospel of Philip, but this is the most penetrating use of it.

2b Those who inherit the dead are themselves dead, and so they inherit those dead. Those who inherit the living are alive and they inherit the living one along with those who are dead. These dead do not inherit anything, for how can someone who is dead inherit the dead? If he who is dead inherits the living he shall not die, but the dead shall be alive.⁵

3a A gentile cannot die, for he is not alive so that he is able to die. Whoever has believed in the truth has lived, and so is in danger of dying.⁶ For since the day that Christ came, the world is created, the cities are decorated, the dead are carried out.⁷

**8** Elsewhere in the Gospel of Philip, "mother" refers to the holy spirit and "father" is, of course, used for God the father. Yet we cannot assume throughout the Gospel of Philip that these words always refer to God and the holy spirit. For this reason, terms like *father* are not capitalized in this translation. Philip tells us that Hebrews only have mothers. On some level, this may make reference to the tradition that Jewish descent is only passed on through the mother. Thus, someone who has a Jewish mother and a gentile father is a Jew, but someone who has a Jewish father and a gentile mother is not a Jew. Also, the first-century Hellenistic Jewish philosopher Philo of Alexandria commented that "the whole nation of the Jews may be looked upon in the light of orphans, if they are compared with all other nations in other lands."

In the Gospel of Thomas 105, Jesus tells us that "whoever knows the father and the mother will be called the son of a whore." According to Thomas, most people would not know the father and mother and could therefore be considered orphans. Anyone who actually does know the father and mother is criticized by others as being worse than an orphan.

**9** These images of gentiles, proselytes, Hebrews and Christians, slaves and sons, the dead and the living accumulate. They are stacked one onto another, paralleling each other, amplifying the imagery. We have to feel that Philip is less concerned with the literal meaning of these statements than with their value as spiritual metaphors. The parallels are not always exact. We might summarize them in the following statements, some of which seem to contradict each other: a gentile is dead; a proselyte cannot convert others, but a Hebrew can; a Hebrew has only a mother, but a Christian has a father and a mother; the son inherits through the father, but the slave doesn't inherit; those who believe in truth are alive, and the living inherit the living. Perhaps this gives us a hierarchy of gentile→proselyte→Hebrew→Christian. In attempting to make a coherent system out of the Gospel of Philip's metaphors, we have to take into account that Philip is an anthology, and these statements are excerpted from different texts. It is also possible that the extracts are being used by Philip to make his own points, which are not necessarily identical to the points made by the original texts.

3b In the days when we used to be Hebrews, we were orphans, brought about through our mother only,[8] but as Christians we have both father and mother.[9]

**10** Now the imagery has shifted from that of religious distinctions and family to the natural world and the seasons. The Coptic word *aion* is a borrowing from the Greek, which may be literally translated as "an age." In Gnostic literature, the aeon is a technical term, sometimes defined as "the realm of eternity." We are told that the winter is the world, the summer is the other aeon. We should not pray or reap in the winter, since we are trying to leave the winter. This is quite similar to the Gospel of Thomas 57 (also in Matthew and Mark) where the weeds planted in the night by the enemy should only be pulled up on the day of harvest, not before. All of our efforts should be ideally directed toward obtaining the state of summer or harvest, which is the other aeon, and not spent on things in this world. The other aeon would not seem to be something that comes to us after death, but something that we can experience in this life.

**11** Being ransomed and redeemed, being saved and atoned for, are part of the technical language of Christianity. They are also attributes of Jesus: the redeemer, the savior, the one who atones. Some of these terms are so familiar to anyone with a background in Christianity that their meaning remains unexplored, and on the other hand so foreign to anyone without that background that it is worth taking some time to explain them.

**12** In modern usage, if you are ransomed, it means that you have been captured and imprisoned as a hostage and that someone has paid to have you released. This is essentially the meaning behind redemption, which can also be rendered as ransom. In the Hebrew Bible, this is most often referred to when a family member or friend pays someone else's debt to a creditor. The debtor's property may have been seized (and "seized" or "captured" are common words in the Gospel of Philip), or the debtor may have been imprisoned. If no relative was available to redeem the person, then the king could step forward, and failing the king, God. These are the roots of these terms. In conventional Christianity, Christ redeems man by his death, so his death is considered a

*(continued on page 12)*

4 Those who sow in the winter reap in the summer. The winter is the world, the summer is the other aeon. Let us sow in the world so that we shall reap in the summer. It is not right for us to pray in the winter. If someone emerges from the winter, then it is the summer. If someone reaps in the winter he will not reap but uproot, and this will not produce fruit. Not only will it come forth [...], but in the other sabbath it will not be fruitful harvest.[10]

5 Christ came to ransom some people, to save others, and to atone yet others.[11] He ransomed those who were strangers and made them his own.[12] And he brought back his own, whom he had given as hostage. Not only did he lay down his soul when he appeared, as he wished, but he had laid it down since the day that the world began. Then he came to take it back, since it had been laid down as a deposit. It had fallen into the hands of thieves and they had captured it. Yet he saved it and ransomed both the evil and the good in this world.

payment made to free man from the debt of sin. We might say that God or Christ redeems from debt in the same way that he frees from slavery. A redeemer figure is very common in Gnostic literature.

The Hebrew word for atonement, *yĕkappēr*, literally means "to cover up." The ritual of atonement involved the scapegoat being loaded with the sins of the people and sent out into the desert. The English word *atonement* is interesting since it literally means "at one."

13  Elaine Pagels reads this passage as representing a different approach to morality. According to Pagels, Philip is suggesting that "what we identify as opposites—'light and dark, life and death, good and evil'—are in reality pairs of interdependent terms in which each implies the other."

14  Another reading could interpret this passage as stating that basic aspects of biological life—breathing, moving, eating, reproducing—cannot be equated with spiritual life, nor can literal death, which is the death of the physical body, be equated with spiritual death, which is the absence of the spirit. Similarly, both "good" and "evil" may have esoteric and literal meanings.

15  It is not quite clear how the concluding two sentences of this section relate to the previous sentences. They would seem to suggest that notions such as good and evil, right and left are impermanent and can therefore be "dissolved" since they belong to this world. Whatever is above this world is eternal.

16  The name that we give to something is not the thing itself, it is just a label. Once a word has been attached to something, the name takes on a life of its own; it may be used in inappropriate ways and even come to refer to something entirely different. This is especially true of esoteric matters. Philip tells us that the usual notion of God is wrong and refers to something that doesn't actually exist. The external understanding of these concepts takes over from the esoteric or inner understanding. Rather than understanding God as referring to some kind of internal spiritual experience, divinity is sought in external things. Philip later gives us more examples of this kind of wrong thinking.

6 Light and darkness, life and death, right and left, are brothers of each other.¹³ It is not possible to separate them from each other. So, those who are good are not good, those who are evil are not evil, nor is life really life, nor death really death.¹⁴ Thus, each shall be dissolved into what it was at the beginning. Yet those who are exalted above the world cannot be dissolved, and are eternal.¹⁵

7 Names given to the worldly are a source of confusion, for they turn hearts away from what really exists, and make them think of that which does not exist.¹⁶ So then someone who thinks of God does not think of what really exists, but of something that doesn't actually exist. So also with the father and the son, and the holy spirit, and with life and light, and the resurrection and the church, and with all of the others. They are made to think not of what exists, but of what does not exist, though these things could point to things that really exist. The names that are in this world confuse, but if the names came from the aeon they could not be used in the world, nor would they have been assigned to worldly things. Their purpose lies in the eternal aeon.

**17** The name that the father is giving the son is not, as might appear at first glance, the son's own name, but the father's name. The unutterable name of God has a considerable body of tradition in later Judaism. God's name was written only using the consonants YHWH, and the vowels were not transmitted textually, so the pronunciation of the name was treated as a great secret. A sixth-century Jewish text, *Toledot Yeshu,* includes a fascinating account, part parody, part tradition, of how Jesus obtained the ineffable name of God. Jesus sneaked into the Temple and wrote down the name of God, which was written on the Temple's foundation stone. When anyone who learned the name left the Temple, two brass lions would roar and the name would be forgotten, so Jesus wrote the name on a piece of parchment and sewed it into his thigh. When he left the Temple and the lions roared he forgot the name, but he was then able to read the piece of parchment. According to the text, this was the source of his magical powers.

**18** Possession of the name of the father can transform a son into a father. Those who have the name of the father no longer seek for the truth but have found it.

**19** The purpose of all these terms and names is to guide us to the truth. There is only one truth, but we need to approach it through many different forms because we are in the world. We should remember that the Gospel of Philip is guiding us to truth, and the text, with all of its fascination and obscurities, is just a set of signposts on the way.

**20** The "archons" or "rulers" occupy a considerable place in Gnostic literature. They are represented as demonic powers who seek to keep humanity trapped in this world. The Nag Hammadi text Hypostasis of the Archons, or the Reality of the Rulers, points out that Paul, whom Gnostics called the great apostle, told us that "our contest is not against flesh and blood; rather, the authorities [rulers or archons] of the universe and the spirits of wickedness" (Eph. 6:12). The Gnostic idea of archons or rulers goes back to the earliest Christianity.

*(continued on page 16)*

8 There is a single name which is not uttered in the world: the name which the father gave to the son. It is placed above every other, for it is the name of the father.17 For the son would not become the father unless he had taken on the name of the father. Those who have this name know it but do not speak it. Those who do not have it cannot even think of it.18 But truth brought names into the world for our sakes, and one cannot refer to truth without names. Truth is single, but its names are many for our sakes, to teach us lovingly this one thing through many things.19

9 The rulers wished to deceive mankind, since they perceived that it was related to what was truly good. So they took the names of the good things and applied them to what is not good, to deceive humanity by the names, and bind them to what is not good. And then what a favor they did for them, they removed them from what is not good and replaced them among the good. They knew what they were doing, for they wanted to take the free man and make him a slave forever.20

In this passage in the Gospel of Philip, the rulers have used names to prevent people from being free. They seem to have reversed the use of these names, so a name that referred to something good now refers to something that is not good, and vice versa.

**21** The powers in this case seem to be pagan gods. Some Christians of the time held that these gods were not just imaginary creations but were real entities, and so they must actually have been demons. Many pagan gods—the Egyptian gods, for example—were depicted as being in animal form, or as being a composite creature with the head or body of an animal and the rest human.

**22** Ancient temples doubled as abbatoirs, since in the ancient world meat was almost always dedicated to a god before slaughter. (This was also true of the Jerusalem Temple while it was still standing, particularly at Passover.) Living animals were killed for the gods, which means that they are no longer alive but are dead. On the other hand, people who offer themselves to God undergo the reverse of this. They were previously (spiritually) dead, and now God has made them alive. This is a spiritual resurrection. This section develops a clever contrast between the literal and metaphorical.

**23** Philip displays a fascination with the appropriate kinds of food (see also section 100). What is food for animals is not appropriate food for humans. The appropriate food for humans comes from Christ, and the bread from heaven reminds us of Moses and the manna in the wilderness. Bread probably refers to spiritual teaching.

*We hope you will enjoy this book and that you will find it useful and use it to enrich your life.*

Book title:

Your comments:

How you learned of this book:

Reasons why you bought this book: (check all that apply) ☐ SUBJECT ☐ AUTHOR ☐ ATTRACTIVE COVER
☐ ATTRACTIVE INSIDE ☐ RECOMMENDATION OF FRIEND ☐ RECOMMENDATION OF REVIEWER ☐ GIFT

If purchased: Bookseller _____ City _____ State _____

**Please send me a SkyLight Paths Publishing catalog.** I am particularly interested in: (check all that apply)

1. ☐ Spirituality
2. ☐ Mysticism/Meditation
3. ☐ Philosophy/Theology
4. ☐ Spiritual Texts
5. ☐ Religious Traditions (Which ones?)
6. ☐ Children's Books
7. ☐ Prayer/Worship
8. ☐ (Other)

Name (PRINT) _____ Phone _____

Street _____ E-mail _____

City _____ State _____ Zip _____

**Please send a SkyLight Paths Publishing catalog to my friend:**

Name (PRINT) _____ Phone _____

Street _____

City _____ State _____ Zip _____

## SkyLight Paths Publishing

Sunset Farm Offices, Rte. 4 • P.O. Box 237 • Woodstock, VT 05091 • Tel: (802) 457-4000 • Fax: (802) 457-4004
**Available at better booksellers. Visit us online at www.skylightpaths.com**

10 There are powers that capture men, not wanting them to be saved, so that they [...] For if a man is saved there will not be any sacrifices, and animals will not be offered up to the powers. Indeed, those to whom offerings were made were animals themselves.21 They were offered up alive, but once they were offered up they became dead. Yet men were offered up dead unto God, and became alive.22

11 Before Christ came, there was no bread in the world. It was just as it was in the garden, where Adam was, where there were many plants as nourishment for animals, but no wheat as food for mankind, so people ate like the animals. But when Christ, the perfect man, came, he brought bread from heaven so that mankind might be fed with the food of man.23

**24** The rulers or archons only have limited power. They are nothing in comparison with higher powers such as the holy spirit or the father. In a fragment quoted by Clement of Alexandria, Valentinus tells us that the heart "is impure by being the habitation of many demons, until it experiences forethought. But when the father, who alone is good, visits the heart, he makes it holy and fills it with light." So we may be justified in interpreting the rulers as the elements of a human being that are not concerned with spiritual matters. If we have a connection to the holy spirit, then these rulers will unwittingly do the bidding of the spirit.

**25** When we read a spiritual text or hear of a teaching, truth is sown in us. These teachings have existed as long as human culture has. The metaphor of sowing relates this directly to the parable of the sower, where the Word is the seed, and those who hear it receive it in different ways. Truth can only be reaped once harvest time has come. Section 4 contains some directions as to what the harvest is, and under what conditions the harvest can be reaped. Few people actualize a teaching, and from another point of view, many are called but few are chosen.

12 The rulers thought that it was by their own power and will that they did what they did. But the holy spirit was hiddenly accomplishing everything through them, as she wished.[24]

13 Truth, which has existed from the beginning, is sown everywhere. Many see it sowed, but few see it reaped.[25]

26 This points out the obvious: since the holy spirit is female, she is unlikely to have impregnated Mary. Spirit is female in Hebrew and Coptic, but neuter in Greek and masculine in Latin. The trinity of father, holy spirit, and son is thus a family unit of father, mother, and child, which is considerably more balanced than the entirely masculine trinity of later Christianity. Although the feminine character of the holy spirit was lost, the Virgin Mary acquired something of the role of the feminine holy spirit.

27 In the mythological narrative of the Nag Hammadi text Hypostasis of the Archons, or the Reality of the Rulers, Eve becomes pregnant with Norea, after bearing Seth: "And she said, 'He has begotten on me a virgin as an assistance for many generations of mankind.' *She* [Norea] *is the virgin whom the forces did not defile.*" (My emphasis.) The presence of Norea in the world begins to act against the rulers, and Norea calls down an angel of the holy spirit and works toward the salvation of mankind. The very similar wording in the Gospel of Philip, and the previous references to the rulers, suggests that Mary might have had a similar role with respect to the holy spirit and the rulers.

28 The apostles and apostolic men are here spoken of negatively, along with the Hebrews. Elsewhere in Philip, the apostles are spoken of approvingly. Philip, whose name gives us the title of this text, is specifically mentioned as an apostle. There may have been political differences between those who claimed descent from the apostles and those who relied on their own spiritual authority. Those who claim spiritual inheritance chiefly through their connection with a teacher and his students, and hence his students' students, and so on—what is called the apostolic succession in the church—tend to rely on the mechanism of transmission and the borrowed authority that this implies, and hence ignore the direct revelation of the spirit. The Valentinians could claim apostolic succession from Paul through Theudas and Valentinus, since Valentinus was said to be a student of Theudas. Paul himself is

*(continued on page 22)*

14 Some say that Mary conceived by the holy spirit. They are wrong. They do not know what they say. Whenever did a woman conceive by another woman?26 Mary is the virgin whom no power has defiled.27 She is a curse to the Hebrews, the apostles and the apostolic men.28 The virgin who has been defiled by no power [...] the powers defile themselves.

an interesting case, since he never met Jesus and spent only a limited amount of time with other apostles. This section possibly also reflects the differing opinions between the Eastern Valentinians in Syria, Egypt, and elsewhere and the Western Valentinians in Europe, centering on Rome. According to the church father Irenaeus, the Eastern branch of Valentinians apparently accepted that Jesus was conceived by the holy spirit. The Western branch was adoptionist, proposing that Jesus was adopted as the son of God at his baptism in the Jordan.

**29** There are two possible meanings to this. One is that Joseph was Jesus's natural father and that God was his spiritual father. The spirit cannot be his father because the spirit, according to the previous section, is female. Alternatively—and this is less likely—this *may* be a reference to the Gnostic notion of there being two gods, the true father and the demiurge who created this world. Classic Gnostic mythology describes how the material world was created by the demiurge (craftsman), a being—often called Yaldabaoth—who was conceived as a result of Wisdom's separation from God. The demiurge, ignorant of the true father, considered himself to be God and is the God worshiped by external forms of religion. The true father is unknown to the world, and knowledge of the father is the goal of the Gnostic.

**30** Literally, the father's house would be the Temple in Jerusalem. But the father's house may also be the "house not made of hands," an internal and spiritual "house." The Temple can also be seen metaphorically, as we shall encounter in section 68. The quoted words in this section are presented as a saying of Jesus. The sayings that survive outside the canonical gospels are known as agrapha, unwritten things, because they were not written down in the New Testament. Of course, we know of these sayings because they are written down elsewhere, so agrapha is a somewhat prejudiced and redundant term.

**31** See the note to section 40 for more of the Gospel of Philip's speculation over the meaning of the names of Jesus. These are part of Philip's overall concern over the use and abuse of names.

15 The Lord would not have said, "my father who is in the heavens," if he did not have another father. Instead he would have simply said, "my father."[29]

16 The Lord said to the disciples, "Take from every house, gather into the father's house, but do not steal when you are in the father's house, and do not take anything out of the father's house.[30]

17 "Jesus" is a hidden name, "Christ" is a revealed name. Thus "Jesus" does not occur in any language, but rather he is called "Jesus" because it is his name. But "Christ" in Syriac is "messiah," and in Greek "Christos," and the others have it according to their own language. "The Nazarene" is the revealed form of the hidden name.[31]

**32** A brief and mysterious saying. Christ is seemingly the most important element, and even includes the father within him.

**33** The saying breaks off midsentence. The common notion of resurrection is of a bodily resurrection, either of Christ's returning from the dead after his crucifixion, or of a general resurrection at the end of time. Celsus, a pagan philosopher of the second century CE who wrote an attack on Christianity that survives partially in the Christian Platonist theologian Origen's third-century response to it, called bodily resurrection a disgusting doctrine. "The soul may have everlasting life, but corpses, as Heraclitus said, 'ought to be thrown away as worse than dung.'"

Those who maintain the idea of a bodily resurrection, where Christ died and then arose from the dead, his crucified body walking away from the tomb, are here said to be confused. But in what way could the Lord have risen before he died? This surely can only be a resurrection of the spirit, from the spiritual death in which humanity finds itself. The Lord rose from the dead spiritually and then died physically. Anyone whose spirit is alive when they die—and according to the Gospel of Philip, this is not true of all of humanity—will survive death.

**34** The body is the vessel of the soul, a fleshly box that can hold divinity. Note that the soul is referred to here, not the spirit. This is not the fallen soul, but the soul that has connection to the spirit and is returning to the father.

**35** In the imagery of the Gnostics and the New Testament, one can put on, or wear, different types of garments, which represent different spiritual states. For instance, one can put on the new or perfect man, or the spirit, or conversely put off the body. As an extension of this form of imagery, when one takes off a piece of clothing one is naked. The attitude to nakedness in Philip and other texts can seem contradictory, yet it depends what kind of nakedness is being referred to. It is better to be naked than to be wearing the wrong kind of psychological clothes. Yet it is better to be clothed with the spirit than it is to be naked. As the Apocryphon of James puts it, "From now I shall unclothe myself in order that I may be clothed."

**18** Christ has everything within him: man, angel, and mystery, and also the father.<sup>32</sup>

**19** Those who say that the Lord first died and then arose are confused, for he first arose and then died. Anyone who first acquires the resurrection shall not die. As God lives, that one would [...] <sup>33</sup>

**20** No one will hide a thing of great value in something that is also of great value, but often someone has put into a thing worth only a penny things whose worth is numbered in the myriads. This is so with the soul. A thing of such great value was put into a humble body.<sup>34</sup>

**21a** Some are afraid that when they arise they will be naked. Because of this, they wish to rise in the flesh, and they do not know that those who wear the flesh are naked themselves. Those who are made into light are stripping themselves naked, they are not being stripped by someone else.<sup>35</sup>

**36** The saying about flesh and blood comes from Paul, 1 Corinthians 15:50. What follows is an extended meditation on what this actually means, what flesh is and what blood is.

**37** John 6:53–54, "So Jesus said to them, 'Truly, truly, I say to you, unless you eat the flesh of the Son of man and drink his blood, you have no life in you; he who eats my flesh and drinks my blood has eternal life, and I will raise him up at the last day.' "

**38** Flesh and blood are allegorized as the Word and the holy spirit. While literal flesh and blood cannot inherit the kingdom, the Word and the holy spirit surely can.

**39** The Gospel of Philip describes two points of view concerning the flesh, and rising up, that are considered to be wrong. The paradox is that the flesh itself does not rise, since what rises is spiritual, yet it is only when we are in the flesh, embodied in the physical world, than we can rise up, out of it.

However, the text here is very confusing, and all of the major scholarly translators have different opinions as to what is being stated. I have adopted Isenberg's reading as a basis for my translation here.

**40** Again, this is another clever contrast between the literal implications of an image, in this case the wearing of garments and its metaphorical usage. Of course, the clothes do not make the man, and a human being is worth much more than a set of clothes. But when the clothes can represent the spirit, or Christ, then those clothes are obviously worth more than the human being.

**21b** Flesh and blood cannot inherit the kingdom of God. What is this thing that shall not inherit? That which is upon all of us. Yet what *shall* inherit is this—that which belongs to Jesus and his blood.[36]

So he says, "He who eats not of my flesh and drinks not of my blood does not have my life within him."[37] What is his flesh? It is the Word, and his blood is the holy spirit. He who has received this has food and drink and clothing.[38] I myself rebuke those others who say that they shall not arise. Both of the following are in error: You who say that the flesh shall not arise, tell me what will arise? You who say that the spirit is in the flesh and the other light is in the flesh. Isn't this also a fleshly statement? For whatever you say, you are stating nothing that is outside of the flesh. It is necessary to arise within this flesh, since everything exists within it.[39]

**21c** In this world, those who wear garments are better than the garments. In the kingdom of heaven, the clothes are superior to those who wear them.[40]

**41** The theme of hidden and the revealed occurs throughout the Gospel of Philip and is also a fundamental theme in the Gospel of Thomas, where we are promised that "what is hidden shall be revealed" (saying 5). In this case, it would seem to refer to hidden significances. Bentley Layton suggests that the "water within water" is baptismal water, since the chrism, which has the same root as Christ, relates to the sacrament of anointing. Yet chrism in some way has fire in it, but water has only water in it.

**42** This passage refers to what is commonly known as the transfiguration scene in the Gospel of Mark and its parallels, where Peter, John, and James go up a high mountain with Jesus and see him speak with Moses and Elijah. There are also other examples of Jesus on the mountain in Gnostic texts.

**43** The Eucharist is the Lord's supper, the partaking of bread and wine that has been part of Christianity since the earliest times. It is possible that the words given here were actually spoken during Valentinian celebrations of the Eucharist. In any case, a second-century version of the Eucharist was very likely to have been less formal than the modern tradition. Some comparison is being made between, on the one hand, the perfect light and the holy spirit and, on the other, the angels and the images. There is probably little difference between the perfect light and the holy spirit.

22 Through water and fire, which purify the whole place, the visible is revealed by the visible, and the hidden made secret by the hidden. Some things are hidden by visible things. There is water within water, there is fire within chrism.[41]

23 Jesus took them all by stealth, for he did not reveal himself as he is, but he has revealed himself in a way in which he is able to be seen within. He revealed himself to them all. He revealed himself to the great as one who is great, to the small as one who is small, to the angels as an angel and to humanity as a man. Thus, his Word concealed him from everyone. Some saw him thinking that they will see their own selves. But when he revealed himself to his disciples on the mountain, he was not small. He became great, and he has made the disciples great, so that they shall be permitted to see him as a great one.[42]

24 He says today in the Eucharist, "You who have united the perfect light with the holy spirit, unite also our angels with the images."[43]

44  A lamb is an image of meekness and of someone who can follow the shepherd. This is similar to the Gospel of John 10:1–3: "Truly, truly, I say to you, he who does not enter the sheepfold by the door but climbs in by another way, that man is a thief and a robber; but he who enters by the door is the shepherd of the sheep. To him the gatekeeper opens; the sheep hear his voice, and he calls his own sheep by name and leads them out."

H. V. Morton, who traveled in Palestine in the 1930s, describes seeing an Arab shepherd in Palestine: "He never drives them as our shepherds drive their sheep. He always walks at their head, leading them along the roads and over the hill to new pasture … the sheep follow their shepherds like dogs." This ancient tradition makes the image of a sheep following a shepherd more comprehensible than does the modern Western method of driving sheep using a dog or a truck. *Lamb,* in this section, and *king,* in the next, are both epithets of Jesus, as in "Lamb of God" and "King of Kings." They have very different implications since a lamb is expected to follow and a king to rule.

45  Some scholars emend "gate" to "king" in line with the following saying, but the text has "gate" and makes perfect sense in that context.

46  If we take this literally, we are sure to agree with it: anyone who goes to see a king should put some clothes on. This is indisputable, a useful piece of advice, and underscores the fact that we will get very little out of the Gospel of Philip if we take it literally. One must be clothed in the right garments, must put on Christ or the spirit.

25 Do not disdain the lamb,[44] for without him it is not possible to see the gate.[45]

26 No one who is naked can go in to see the king.[46]

**47** The sons of Adam (the earthly man) are those who are born, grow like grass, and die. Those who are of heaven are continually being born, continually renewing their spirits, and being born again from the spirit. The Dialogue of the Savior, another of the immensely valuable texts found at Nag Hammadi, contains the following amplification of this:

Matthew said, "Tell me, Lord, how the dead die, and how the living live."

The Lord said, "You have asked me about a saying [...] which eye has not seen, nor have I heard it, except from you. But I say to you that when what invigorates a man is removed, he will be called 'dead.' And when what is alive leaves what is dead, what is alive will be called upon."

Judas said, "Why else, for the sake of truth, do they die and live?"

The Lord said, "Whatever is born of truth does not die. Whatever is born of woman dies."

**48** If a son is still a child, then he cannot procreate and so cannot yet father sons himself. But if his father continues to beget new sons, then he can acquire new brothers. It is stretching the metaphor a bit to suggest that he is "begetting" them as brothers. Perhaps this is about each of us having to go back to the source, the father, and becoming one with the father, and so refers to the difference between psychics, who are identified with the soul, and pneumatics, who have spirit. The son who cannot beget a son takes us directly back to the proselyte who cannot make other proselytes.

27a The sons of the man of heaven are more numerous than those of the man of earth. If the sons of Adam are so numerous, even though they die, how many are the sons of the perfect man? These do not die but they are continually being born.[47]

27b The father creates a son, yet it is not possible for someone who is begotten to beget others—instead, the son begets brothers not sons.[48]

**49** This is a straight contrast between being born physically and being born again, or born from above. This has remained a popular metaphor in Christianity, and nowadays Christian converts from a variety of denominations call themselves "born-again Christians." The Gospel of John contains the most famous use of this term. That gospel labors the point in the account of Nicodemus in John 3, in which Nicodemus has a great deal of difficulty in understanding the idea of a second birth: "Jesus answered him, 'Very truly, I tell you, no one can see the kingdom of God without being born from above.' Nicodemus said to him, 'How can anyone be born after having grown old? Can one enter a second time into the mother's womb and be born?' Jesus answered, 'Very truly, I tell you, no one can enter the kingdom of God without being born of water and Spirit. What is born of the flesh is flesh, and what is born of the Spirit is spirit'" (4–6).

Parts of this excerpt from the Gospel of John would not look at all out of place in Philip. The second birth is clearly the birth of the spirit, just as the first birth is the birth of the physical body. The canonical status of John means that Christians read it and take it seriously, but the same people would be likely to dismiss this passage as Gnostic and inauthentic if they found it in the Gospel of Philip.

**50** Being nourished from the mouth is an odd kind of imagery that refers to the mouth being the producer of speech, and hence being nourished from the mouth means taking in teaching as if it is a kind of food, which it is. It derives from an ancient idiom such as Numbers 12:8, "With him I speak mouth to mouth, clearly, and not in dark speech; and he beholds the form of the LORD." The Gospel of Thomas 108 has a clear example of this. Jesus says, "Whoever drinks from my mouth will be like me. I will become him, and what is hidden will be revealed to him."

27c All those who are begotten in the world are begotten in nature, and the others are nourished from the place from which they have been born.[49] Man receives nourishment from the promise of the place above, [...] from the mouth, where the Word came out, he would be nourished from the mouth and become perfect.[50]

51   The Valentinian Tripartite Tractate, from the Nag Hammadi codices, has "Those which exist have come forth from the Son and the Father like kisses, because of the multitude of some who kiss one another with a good, insatiable thought, the kiss being a unity, although it involves many kisses."

52   In the original Coptic, this actually says "*her* sister." This is generally emended to *his* sister, that is, Jesus's sister, since the church father Epiphanius tells us that Jesus's sister was called Mary. If we leave this as *her* sister, then Mary's sister is also called Mary.

53   In the Gospel of John, three Marys and an unnamed aunt of Jesus are at the foot of the cross. "Near the cross of Jesus stood his mother, his mother's sister, Mary the wife of Clopas, and Mary Magdalene" (John 19:25). The three Marys are a popular image in Christianity and have inspired many paintings. This section of the Gospel of Philip has acquired particular notoriety due to the theories that Jesus was married to Mary Magdalene. It is difficult to think that this is meant to be taken literally, or that this should be taken as having any verifiable historical basis. The Gospel of Philip seems to be pointing out how odd it is that each of the women is called Mary. And what are they doing, all three of them at all times walking around with the Lord? Mary is the *koinonos* of Jesus. This is a loanword from Greek, and its meanings include "companion" or "partner," but not necessarily in a sexual sense. That Mary Magdalene is the companion of Jesus is more likely to be something along the lines of the mythical pairing of Christ and the holy spirit, or of the savior and Sophia that occur in other Valentinian texts.

27d The perfect are conceived through a kiss. Thus we shall kiss each other. We receive conception from the grace which is in each of us.[51]

28 There were three Marys who walked with the Lord at all times: his mother and his sister[52] and the Magdalene, who is called his companion. So his mother and sister and companion are called "Mary."[53]

54  R. McL. Wilson, one of the major early Gospel of Philip specialists, pointed out that, in Coptic as in English, "father" and "son" are indeed single words, and "holy spirit" is a double word, because it consists of two words. But this doesn't seem to be what the passage is getting at. Somehow the terms *father* and *son* apply to both earth and heaven, whereas *holy spirit* is revealed on earth and hidden in heaven. Perhaps this is to do with "father" and "son" having both literal and metaphorical meanings, unlike "holy spirit."

55  Evil powers or rulers are also tricked by the holy spirit in section 12. The "mother" referred to here must be the holy spirit.

56  The use of a symbol generally depends on its natural properties. Salt is a particularly complex substance in this sense: salt land is barren ("the whole land thereof is brimstone, and salt, and burning, that it is not sown, nor beareth, nor any grass groweth therein," Deuteronomy 29:23 tells us) and salt water undrinkable, yet consuming salt is essential for human existence, and salt has always been a valuable commodity. Salt is also used to preserve food and to hold off corruption.

This section suggests both that Wisdom is barren, due to the analogy with salt land, and that Wisdom is essential for an offering, in the same way that salt is essential for food. Reference is also made to the canonical gospels: "For every one shall be salted with fire, and every sacrifice shall be salted with salt. Salt is good: but if the salt have lost his saltiness, wherewith will ye season it? Have salt in yourselves, and have peace one with another" (Mark 9:45–50).

29 The father and the son are single names,
the holy spirit is a double name. For the former
are everywhere, in the heavens and in the earth;
they are in the hidden and in the revealed. But the
holy spirit is revealed in the earth and hidden
in heaven.[54]

30 Those who are holy are served by the evil
powers, for the powers are blinded through the holy
spirit so that they think they are serving a man,
when in fact they are working for the holy ones.
Because of this, a disciple one day made a request of
the Lord for something of this world. He said to
him, "Ask your mother, and she will give you what
belongs to another."[55]

31 The apostles said to the disciples, "May our
offering have salt." They called Wisdom salt, for no
offering is acceptable if it lacks her. Yet Wisdom is
barren if she has no son. So she is called [...] salt.
Wherever they will be [...] in their own way [...]
she makes many sons.[56]

**57** This is something of a repetition of section 2 above and is a confirmation that the Gospel of Philip is an anthology of excerpts from other texts. The thought expressed in this section derives directly from Paul in Galatians 4: "I mean that the heir, as long as he is a child, is no better than a slave, though he is the owner of all the estate; but he is under guardians and trustees until the date set by the father. So with us; when we were children, we were slaves to the elemental spirits of the universe."

From the point of view of the Gospel of Philip, Paul must be speaking about the rulers or archons when he talks of the elemental spirits of the universe.

**58** In the midst of all this commentary, we should stand back for a moment and appreciate the poetry here: "By the same breath, the fire blazes, is fanned and is blown out." There is a play on words here based on multiple meanings of the Greek word *pneuma*. *Pneuma* can mean "spirit" and "breath" and "wind," so we could read this as "By the same spirit the fire blazes, is fanned and is blown out."

**59** This is another piece of wordplay based on similarities between two Semitic words. The previous section depended on Greek for its wordplay. *Echamoth* is derived from the biblical Hebrew word for wisdom, *hokhmoth*. *Echmoth* is from *ech-moth*, which means "like death" in Aramaic and Hebrew. This wordplay is used to contrast true wisdom and the wisdom of this world, which is the wisdom of the dead.

**60** Tame animals serve man, and this benefits both man and the animals, since the latter are cared for and receive food. This is elaborated upon, until Philip tells us that the animals should be equated with powers. The relationship between the perfect man and the powers or animals is like the relationship between the holy spirit and the rulers or powers, which is also detailed in sections 12 and 30.

32 What belongs to the father belongs to the son. As long as the son is small, his own things are not entrusted to him. When he becomes a man, his father gives him everything that belongs to him.[57]

33 Those who go astray are begotten by the spirit, and they also go astray through her. By the same breath, the fire blazes, is fanned and is blown out. [58]

34 Echamoth is one thing and Echmoth is another. Echamoth is simply wisdom, but Echmoth is the wisdom of the dead. This wisdom which is the dead wisdom is called the lesser wisdom.[59]

35 There are animals which submit to man, such as calves, asses and others of this kind. There are others that do not submit, and are alone in the wilds. Man ploughs the field using tame animals and through this he feeds himself as well as the animals, whether they submit or not. This is the way of the perfect man; he ploughs through the submissive powers, providing for everything to exist. It is because of this that the whole place stands in rest, whether good or evil, or of the right or the left. The holy spirit shepherds everyone and commands all of the powers, the submissive and unsubmissive. For she encloses them within so that they will not be able to escape.[60]

**61** Adam is "modeled" in that he was molded out of earth. Because he is molded from earth, he is not begotten by God and is not a son of God. And because he is not a son of God, his own sons are not noble. This is one of a number of ingenious interpretations of Genesis.

**62** In this variant of the birth of Cain, rather than being the son of Adam, Cain is the son of the serpent. This implies that the serpent seduced Eve. It is Cain's status as a son of the serpent that leads him to murder Abel. In other versions of the Gnostic myth, Yaldabaoth, the lion-headed demiurge, seduces Eve.

The Apocryphon of John covers this in elaborate detail: "And the chief archon seduced her and he begot in her two sons; the first and the second (are) Eloim and Yave. Eloim has a bear-face and Yave has a cat-face. The one is righteous but the other is unrighteous. (Yave is righteous but Eloim is unrighteous.) Yave he set over the fire and the wind, and Eloim he set over the water and the earth. And these he called with the names Cain and Abel with a view to deceive."

In Jewish traditions, Samael, a demonic figure who is often equivalent to Satan and who also occurs in Gnostic texts as a name of the demiurge, seduces Eve as a serpent. The Talmud contains rather explicit guidelines for dealing with women who have been, or are about to be, penetrated by snakes.

Adam and Eve had a child Seth who, although he doesn't occur in Philip, is considered a great figure by other Gnostics, and also in other nonbiblical traditions. He represents an uncontaminated line springing from Adam and Eve.

Paul uses the story of Adam and Eve metaphorically, in a way in which the Gospel of Philip would surely approve: "I feel a divine jealousy for you, for I betrothed you to Christ to present you as a pure bride to her one husband. But I am afraid that as the serpent deceived Eve by his cunning, your thoughts will be led astray from a sincere and pure devotion to Christ" (2 Cor. 11:3).

36a Adam was modeled, but you would not find his sons to be beautiful creations. If he had not been made but begotten, his seed would be found to be noble. Yet now he is modeled, and he begets, what nobility is this?[61]

36b First, adultery occurred, afterwards murder. He was begotten in adultery, being the son of a serpent. So he became a murderer like his father and killed his brother. Every coupling that has occurred between those who are not similar to each other is adultery.[62]

**63** In section 47 Jesus is also a dyer. God's dyes are distinctive, in that they go inside and change an individual to the core and do not just dye the surface. These dyes give immortality.

**64** We can experience the outside world through the perceptions of our senses, but the inner world, particularly the world of spiritual states, cannot be studied in this way. The only way that one can understand a spiritual state is by experiencing it, and hence becoming it. As Paul wrote, "But he who is united to the Lord becomes one spirit with him" (1 Cor. 6:16–17).

**65** Here we have a beautiful distinction between love and faith. Faith looks up to what is higher and is thus in a position of receiving. But when we love, we already have something higher within us, and so love can give this out to others. Someone who has not received is a Hebrew, that is, a psychic, not a pneumatic (see note 48 above).

**37** God is a dyer. Just as those good pigments, which are called true, go within the things that are dyed, so it is with those things dyed by God. Because his dyes are immortal, those things are made immortal through his colors. Yet God baptizes what he baptizes in water.[63]

**38** It is impossible for anyone to see the things that really exist unless he becomes like them. It is not so in the world. You can see the sun without becoming a sun, see the sky and the earth and all other things without becoming them. But in the world of truth, if you see anything of that place you become one with what is there. You saw the spirit and you became the spirit; you saw the Christ, you became the Christ; you saw the father, you shall become the father. Thus, in this world you indeed see everything and do not see yourself, but in that other place you do see yourself—and you shall become what you see.[64]

**39** Faith receives, love gives. No one can receive without faith, nor can anyone give without love. We believe so that we shall receive, yet we give so that we shall love. Otherwise, someone who gives without love derives no benefit from having given. Anyone who has not received the Lord is still a Hebrew.[65]

**66** Christ is the Greek translation of the Hebrew *māšîah*. Jesus in Aramaic is Yeshua, a shortened form of Yehoshua, which is translated into English as Joshua, and means "God saves." "Nazara" appears in the New Testament as an unusual form for Nazareth. Nazara does not mean "truth" in Hebrew, Aramaic, or any other language. But the church father Irenaeus mentions that in a formula spoken by Valentinians—"I do not divide the Spirit of Christ, neither the heart nor the supercelestial power which is merciful; may I enjoy Thy name, O Savior of truth!"—"the savior of truth" translates "Jesus Nazaria." The Syriac word for "messiah," *mšīhā,* can also mean "measured." Section 17 also looks at the significance of the names of Jesus.

**67** The pearl is a symbol of what is most precious within one. In nature a pearl forms within an oyster in response to the irritation caused by, for example, a grain of sand, which is itself another common Christian symbol. The pearl of great price in Matthew is perhaps the best-known example of the use of this symbolism. The beautiful and esoteric Gnostic Hymn of the Pearl, which is possibly Valentinian and is contained within the third-century Acts of Thomas, contains one of the most intriguing accounts of the fall of the soul and its return to the father. The church father Irenaeus, the anti-Gnostic who has proved so valuable in preserving information about the Gnostics, wrote: "For even as gold, when submersed in filth, loses not on that account its beauty, but retains its own native qualities, the filth having no power to injure the gold, so they affirm that they cannot in any measure suffer hurt, or lose their spiritual substance, whatever the material actions in which they may be involved."

**68** Christianity was still a new and unknown phenomenon in the second century. It was viewed with suspicion by many, and, internally, Christianity was full of divisions, with a huge variety of sects calling themselves Christian. Greek, Roman, Barbarian, and Jew are fundamentally ethnic categories, whereas Christians could come from any race, nationality, or culture, from slaves or free men and women.

40 The apostles before us called him Jesus the Nasorean, the Christ. The last name is Christ, the first name is Jesus; the middle is the Nazarene. Messiah is a double term, meaning both the Christ and "the measured." Jesus in Hebrew means the "atonement." Nazara is the truth, so the Nazarene is therefore the truth. Christ is what is measured, and the Nazarene and Jesus are those who have measured him.[66]

41 The pearl that has been cast into the muck is not despised, nor if it is anointed with balsam does it become more valued. Instead, it always has great worth to its owner. This is the way of the sons of God: wherever they are, they still have the value given them by their father.[67]

42 If you say, "I am a Jew," no one will be moved. If you say, "I am a Roman," no one will be disturbed. If you say, "I am a Greek, a barbarian, a slave or a free man," no one will be troubled. If you say, "I am a Christian," everyone will take heed. O that I may receive him whose name the world will not be able to endure.[68]

**69** God eats man in the sense that man is consumed in God. Animals are not sacrificed to God but to pagan gods who are not gods. Animal sacrifice never had any part in Christianity, but was a staple of ancient religion, including Judaism during the Temple period. So, from this point of view, Christians sacrifice themselves to God, whereas Jews and pagans sacrificed animals. See also section 10, which deals with a similar notion.

**70** This part of the Gospel of Philip contains a sequence of beautiful and clear parables. An item that has the breath (or spirit) of God in it is remade when it is destroyed. Something without that spirit is just destroyed.

Glass is, of course, more beautiful and, in the ancient world, more precious than earthenware. This surely refers to those who are pneumatics and those who are not, but this is a true parable because it is not allegorized, although it does contain a double meaning. See also section 33 for another play on the double meaning of *pneuma* as spirit and breath.

**71** This parable is obviously about those who turn around in circles of unproductive effort instead of getting somewhere. Even a simple parable like this contains references to "power" and "angel." They seem out of place and may have been added later.

**72** The Gospel of Philip is in Coptic and is most likely a translation from a Greek original, yet it contains comments on the meanings of words in Greek, Syriac, Hebrew, and Aramaic. *Pharisatha* literally means "broken bread" but can also mean "that which is spread out." "Spread out" is commonly used in reference to the crucifixion, the arms being spread out on the cross, for example in Odes of Solomon 35, "And I spread out my hands in the ascent of myself, and I directed myself towards the Most High, and I was redeemed towards Him."

43 God is an eater of men. So man is sacrificed. Before man was sacrificed, animals were. For those to whom they are sacrificed are not gods.[69]

44 Vessels of glass and pottery are usually made by fire. But if glass vessels break they are made again, for they are made by breath. Yet if pottery vessels break they are destroyed, for they came about without breath.[70]

45 A donkey turning a millstone walked a hundred miles. When it was released it was found to still be in the same place. There are many who make journeys and do not get anywhere. When evening came they saw neither city nor village, neither a created thing nor a natural one, neither power nor angel. The wretches toiled in vain.[71]

46 The Eucharist is Jesus. For in Syriac he called it *pharisatha,* which means "to spread out." For Jesus came to crucify the world.[72]

[73] Section 37 also contains a reference to dyeing. The second-century Infancy Gospel of Thomas contains a somewhat similar story, "One day, when Jesus was running about and playing with some children, he passed by the workshop of a dyer called Salem. They had in the workshop many cloths which he had to dye. The Lord Jesus went into the dyer's workshop, took all these cloths and put them into a cauldron full of indigo. When Salem came and saw that the cloths were spoiled, he began to cry aloud and asked the Lord Jesus, saying: 'What have you done to me, son of Mary? You have ruined my reputation in the eyes of all the people of the city; for everyone orders a suitable color for himself, but you have come and spoiled everything.' And the Lord Jesus replied: 'I will change for you the color of any cloth which you wish to be changed,' and he immediately began to take the cloths out of the cauldron, each of them dyed in the color the dyer wished, until he had taken them all out."

[74] The number seventy-two occurs repeatedly in Jewish and Christian tradition. It is traditionally the number of the nations, the different varieties of people who made up the non-Jewish, gentile world. Levi is of course a typical Jewish name. The apostle Matthew is also called Levi, and it is possible, though by no means probable, that this is a reference to him. Matthew was also a significant figure for the Gnostics.

47 The Lord went into the dyeing house of Levi.[73] He took out seventy-two colors[74] and threw them into the vat. He brought all of them out white and said, "Thus has the son of man come as a dyer."

**75** Wisdom is also called barren in section 31.

**76** We actually have a lacuna (gap) in the manuscript where "mouth" has been inserted. While there are anatomically many places where Jesus might have kissed Mary, the mouth is a good bet, not only because people do kiss each other on the mouth, but because this had a symbolic importance. See section 27 for a note on this.

**77** The attention that Jesus gives Mary is perhaps a little similar to the affection between the Beloved Disciple and Jesus in the Gospel of John, or between James and Jesus in the Second Apocalypse of James from the Nag Hammadi library: "And he (Jesus) kissed my mouth. He took hold of me, saying, 'My beloved! Behold, I shall reveal to you those (things) that (neither) [the] heavens nor the archons have known.... '" What is being claimed here for Mary is not any erotic or marital connection to Jesus, but a special position as a disciple. Mary is being compared to the man who can see, whereas the other disciples are being compared to those who are blind. To raise up a particular disciple and put down others is a standard device in early Christian literature.

**78** This saying occurs in other places in Christian literature. Irenaeus has "Fortunate [blessed] is one who existed before being human." But in Philip this may actually be a quotation from the Gospel of Thomas 19, "Blessed is he who exists from the beginning before he comes to be." There are enough sayings in the Gospel of Philip that resemble sayings in the Gospel of Thomas for us to tentatively propose that the Gospel of Thomas was one of the texts that Philip used when he was compiling this anthology.

48 That Wisdom which is called barren is the mother of many angels.75 And the companion of the savior is Mary Magdalene. The Lord loved Mary more than the other disciples and kissed her often on her [mouth].76 The rest of them saw him loving Mary and said to him, "Why do you love her more than us?" The savior replied, "Why do I not love you as I do her? When a blind man and one who can see are both in the dark, they are the same as one another. When the light comes, then he who sees will behold the light and he who is blind will remain in darkness."77

49 The Lord said, "Blessed is he who existed before he came into being. For he who exists, did exist and will exist."78

**79** Although man is not as physically strong as many wild animals, he has an element in the hidden world. Without the presence of man, the animals turn on each other. When man is there, they serve him and receive food for themselves. This connects with other parts of the Gospel of Philip, such as in section 30, where the holy spirit actually controls the powers. See also section 35 for an account of man's dealings with animals. It is an unusual feature of the Gospel of Philip that a number of similar pieces are found throughout the text.

**80** In an immersive baptism, one is dunked under the water and then comes up for air. It is the coming up from the water that is arguably more significant than the going down. A strong experience like baptism can produce a sense of reality being more vivid, and it is possible that this is the experience of the holy spirit. The writer seems to accept that not everyone who is Christian has the holy spirit. In the Gospel of Mark, when Jesus is baptized "as he was coming up out of the water he saw the heavens torn apart and the Spirit descending like a dove upon him" (Mark 1:9).

**81** This is the first reference to the mystery of marriage. Unfortunately, much of this saying is fragmentary. Referring to sex as defilement is a seemingly negative attitude to sex, but it is not clear what this is in reference to, and in general the Gospel of Philip has a healthy attitude toward sex and to marriage in particular. Perhaps it indicates that the act of sex, however beautiful, is a shadow of the real union that can occur in the spiritual bridal chamber. Also, as Philip is an anthology, its different sources can have different points of view.

50 The superiority of man is not revealed, but lies in what is hidden. So he is master of animals who are stronger than him, and are greater in terms of both what is hidden and what is revealed. This allows them to survive. Yet if man is separated from them, they bite and kill each other. They will eat each other because they could not find food. Yet now they have found food because mankind has worked the earth.[79]

51 If someone goes down into the water and comes up without having received anything, and says, "I am a Christian," he has taken the name on loan. Yet if he has the holy spirit, the name is a gift to him. He who has received a gift does not have it taken away, but he who has taken out a loan will have it demanded from him. This is how it is when one experiences a mystery.[80]

52 The mystery of marriage is great. For the world would not exist without it. Now the existence of the world [...] the existence of marriage [...] Consider sexual intimacy [...]

Its image consists of a defilement.[81]

**82** At first glance this might seem to be the product of a somewhat feverish imagination. Unclean spirits are preying on men and women in a way that is reminiscent of the succubi and incubi of medieval legend—demons who would seduce men and women while they were dreaming. The Apocryphon of John has a section where Yaldabaoth sends down angels disguised as men to seduce human women. But the Gospel of Philip is not advocating celibacy as a way out of this. The point is that it is only when a woman or man sits alone that the foolish males and females come and seduce her or him. Putting aside for a moment the question of what might be symbolically male or female, it is only when a man or woman is alone that he or she attracts these unclean spirits. While on the surface, this passage may seem to have a distasteful attitude toward sex, it is actually promoting relationships between men and women.

The Gospel of Philip takes this a step further, as it typically does, and then tells us that the image and the angel should unite, thus throwing into question whether this passage refers to actual men and women at all. The mirrored bridal chamber might sound a bit kinky, but it probably refers to the idea of seeing oneself.

53 Unclean spirits have male and female forms. The males are those who unite with souls which inhabit a female form, the females are those which unite with those in a male form, in an inappropriate way. No one will be able to escape from these once they are received, unless both male and female power are received, when the bridegroom is with the bride. They are received them in the mirrored bridal chamber. Whenever foolish females see a man sitting alone, they leap on him, engage with him and defile him. So also the foolish men, when they see a beautiful woman sitting alone, seduce and coerce her so that they might defile her. Yet if the male and the female are seated together, females are not able to go to the male, nor males to the female. If the image and the angel unite, no one can attempt to get to the male or the female.[82]

**83**  Someone who comes out of the world is presumably in the other aeon, the realm of eternity. Many of the previous themes of the Gospel of Philip are repeated here—the powers, the flesh, unclean spirits, the holy spirit. The key to transcending the flesh is to neither love it nor fear it, and it seems that this can only really be done when one has the holy spirit. From the interleaving of unclean spirits, demons and rulers, and references to the flesh, it would seem that the rulers and all of the others are particularly connected with the body and wish to keep the soul tied to the body.

**84**  The Middle is a technical term in Gnosticism. There is this world, in which we live, and there is the resurrection, to which we aspire, and between them is the Middle. Nothing in this world is truly good or evil, and the resurrection is the place of rest, of what is truly good. Yet the Middle is truly evil. Since this world corresponds to the body, and the resurrection to the spirit, the Middle must correspond to the soul. When we are stripped of the flesh—which in this case refers to physical death—we no longer have a body, so can either find ourselves in the resurrection, which means that we have become spirit, or in the Middle, in which case we would only be soul. For the Gospel of Philip, to die with only a soul and no spirit seems to be the worst thing that can happen to anyone. In other accounts of Valentinianism, particularly Irenaeus's account of Ptolemy's system, Echamoth (Wisdom, see section 34), which Irenaeus spells *Achamoth,* is in the Middle and will eventually enter into Perfection and be united with the savior in the bridal chamber. Since the Middle will then be empty, the demiurge and the psychics will enter the Middle. All this is meant to happen when the spiritual element of the cosmos is perfected.

54 Whoever comes out of the world is not able to be seized any longer because he had been in the world. He is revealed as being above the desires of the flesh. He is master of desire. He is superior to envy. If the rulers come, they capture him and strangle him. How will this one be able to escape the powers? How will he be able to hide from them? Often there are some who come and say, We have faith, in order that [...] the unclean spirits and demons. For if they had the holy spirit, no unclean spirit would cling to them. Do not fear what is in the flesh, nor love it. If you fear it, it will be your master. If you love it, it will devour and strangle you.[83]

55 Either someone exists in this world or in the resurrection or in the Middle. May it not happen that I am found there! This world has good and evil within it. Its good things are not good and its evil things are not evil. But there is an evil after this world that is truly evil, that is, the Middle. It is death. While we are in this world it is right for us to acquire the resurrection, so that when we are stripped of the flesh, we will be found in rest, not traveling in the Middle. For many stray on the way.[84]

**85** Some of the details in this section are rather murky. But the gist of it seems to be connected with the wish to do something (in this case, the wish to come out of the world) and the ability to carry this out. One has to both wish to do something and act on that wish for it to be successful. Perhaps this is discussing something similar to the Epistle of James 2:26 in the New Testament, which argues, "For just as the body without the spirit is dead, so faith without works is also dead."

**86** The left half of the page is missing here. Some words are readable, but the majority of this section of the text is so fragmentary that nothing can be gained by listing possible reconstructions here.

**87** Different metaphors can describe different aspects of spiritual states: if a state is described as light, it evokes a different response in the reader or listener than if it is described as fire. The various physical properties of light and fire give rise to further metaphorical developments. The Gospel of Philip does not make hard and fast distinctions between these metaphors. Fire is chrism, light is fire, and therefore (we might guess) light is also chrism.

56 It is good to come out of the world before someone sins. There are some indeed who neither wish to nor have the ability to. There are others who wish but do not benefit from it, for they did not act on the wish, since [...] they do not act makes them sinners. And if they do not act, righteousness will be hidden from them. And it is always a matter of the wish, not the action.⁸⁵

57 An apostle saw in a vision some people confined in a house of fire and bound with flaming [...]⁸⁶

58 The soul and the spirit have come into being in water and in fire. The son of the bridal chamber has come through water and fire and light. Fire is the chrism, light is the fire. I do not speak of the formless fire, but of the other fire whose form is white and which is made of beautiful light which gives out beauty.⁸⁷

**88** The notions expressed here are fundamental to the Gospel of Philip and tell us how the text should be interpreted: it is truth expressed using types and images. Typology is a form of expression and thinking that was widespread in early Christianity—for instance, events and figures in the Hebrew Bible were seen to prefigure or express the truths of Christianity. When Philip dies on the cross in the third-century Acts of Philip, which is discussed in the introduction, he cries that he "bears the *type* of the first man." The Gospel of Philip's use of Adam and Cain and Abel is an example of typology.

The use of myth, symbol, and allegory to express spiritual truth was an approach that was common throughout the ancient world. The fifth-century Roman writer Macrobius wrote something very similar concerning the Greek mysteries, "Plain and naked exposition of herself is repugnant to nature. She wishes her secrets to be treated by myth. Thus the Mysteries themselves are hidden in the tunnels of figurative expression, so that not even to initiates the nature of such realities may present herself naked, but only an elite may know about the real secret, through the interpretation furnished by wisdom."

The Gospel of Mark tells us, "To you it has been given to know the mystery of the kingdom of God; but to those who are outside, all things come in parables" (Mark 4:11). Gnostics would understand this as referring to the respective understandings of pneumatics and psychics (see note 48 above).

**89** The Gospel of Philip is full of fascinating metaphor and imagery, with complex combinations of symbolism, but it also stresses that this is not the ultimate point of the text. The experience of rebirth is not the same thing as the image of rebirth, which consists merely in talking about rebirth. This intoxicating shower of imagery concludes with a startling statement that anyone who has followed the instructions that are described here is no longer a Christian but a Christ. Paul would have agreed wholeheartedly.

**90** This saying lists all of the sacraments referred to in Philip.

59 Truth did not come into the world naked, but came in types and images. The world cannot receive it in any other way.[88] There is rebirth and an image of rebirth. It is truly necessary to be born again through the image. Which image? Resurrection. The image must rise again through the image. Through the image the bridal chamber and the image must enter into the truth: this is the regeneration. It is appropriate not only for those who produce the name of the father with the son and with the holy spirit, but those also who have really acquired these. If someone has not acquired them, the name will be taken from him. Yet one acquires them in the chrism of the power of the cross.

The apostles called it the power of the right with the left. For someone who has this is no longer a Christian, but a Christ.[89]

60 The Lord did everything in a mystery: a baptism and a chrism and a eucharist and a redemption and a holy bridal chamber.[90]

**91** The Gospel of Thomas 22 also contains this saying: "When you make the two into one, and when you make the inside like the outside, and the outside like the inside, and the above like the below ... " Although the saying never occurs in the canonical gospels, it is one of the most widely attested sayings of Jesus and crops up in a variety of places, such as Clement of Alexandria's quotation from the Gospel of the Egyptians, the Acts of Philip, and the letter of Clement of Rome. The Gospel of Philip adds that making the two into one is achieved by means of types.

**92** The idea that there is a man of heaven and one above him is reminiscent of the Gospel of Thomas 11, where Jesus says, "This heaven will pass away and the one above it will pass away." It is entirely possible that the author of the Gospel of Philip has used the Gospel of Thomas as a source, and perhaps the Gospel of Philip is in contention with the Gospel of Thomas here.

**93** Philip's scheme of the outer, the inner, and the innermost corresponds with body, soul, and spirit. Spirit and father and fullness (the Gnostic term *pleroma*) all seem to be on the same level. A number of quotations from Matthew are included here, all understood in a spiritual sense.

**94** This also has a certain similarity to a saying in the Gospel of Thomas 49: "Blessed are the single ones and the chosen, for you will find the kingdom. For you came out of it and you will go in again."

**95** The separation of the male and female causes death. Since the male and female can reunite, and death shall no longer be, we would be justified in this case to think that this death is a spiritual death—the absence of the spirit in this life—rather than the physical death of the body. Elaine Pagels suggests that it is Eve who represents the spirit and Adam the soul in this case.

61 The Lord said, "I have come to make the below like the above, and the outer like the inner and to unite them in the place by means of types [...]91

Those who say that there is a man of heaven and that there is one above him are wrong, for they call the revealed man of heaven the one who is below and the hidden one the one who is above him.92 For it is better to say the inner, the outer, and what is outside the outer. Thus, the Lord called destruction "the outer darkness." Nothing is outside of it.

He said, "My father who is hidden," he said, "Go into your secret room, shut the door behind you and pray to the father who is hidden." That is, the one who is the innermost. Now, what is innermost of all is the fullness. Beyond that there is nothing further within. This is what is called "He who is above all."93

62 Before Christ came, some came out from a place they are no longer able to go into. Then Christ came; he brought out those who had gone in and brought in those who had gone out.94

63 In the days when Eve was within Adam, death did not exist. When she separated from him, death came into being. If he enters again and takes her to himself, death shall no longer exist.95

**96** This interpretation of Jesus's last words on the cross assumes that God (or the spirit) had already departed from the mortal man Jesus. Just before the third-century pagan philosopher Plotinus died, he said, "I am striving to give back the Divine in myself to the Divine in the All."

**97** This section is too fragmentary to make any sense of.

**98** A free man is of course the opposite of a slave. A virgin has not only not been defiled by the powers (and in section 14 Mary is the virgin that no power has defiled), but a virgin probably still lives with her father.

**99** Both light and water are necessary for baptism. This repeats the theme of section 51, where a true Christian receives the holy spirit during baptism. So we can assume that light (and the chrism) are much the same as the spirit. These disparate elements are joined together in a clever and beautiful image of the need for both light and either water or a mirror to see oneself.

64 "My God, my God, why O Lord have you forsaken me?" He said this on the cross, for he had departed from that place.⁹⁶

65 [...] born through [...] God [...] from the dead [...]⁹⁷

66 The bridal bed is not for animals, nor for slaves nor for defiled women, but rather it is for free men and virgins.⁹⁸

67 We are born again through the holy spirit, but we are begotten by Christ through two things. We are anointed through the spirit. And when we were born we were united.

Without light, no one can see himself in water or in a mirror. Nor can you see by light without water or a mirror. Thus it is appropriate to baptize in both light and water. The light is the chrism.⁹⁹

68 There were three places of sacrifice in Jerusalem: one to the west was holy, another to the south was the holy of the holy, and to the east was the holy of holies where the high priest went. Baptism is the holy place, redemption is the holy of the holy, the holy of the holies is the bridal chamber. Baptism is the resurrection with redemption entering the bridal chamber. Yet the bridal chamber is above these. You will not find anything that compares to it.

(continued on page 69)

**100** The division of the Temple into the holy, the holy of the holy, and the holy of the holies is used to classify the sacraments of baptism, redemption, and the bridal chamber. Baptism seems to be preliminary; redemption probably refers to the buying back of the soul from its debts or its captivity, and in the bridal chamber the soul is united with the spirit. The latter section is obviously similar in theme to the other sections about the Temple and bridal chamber and includes reference to the veil of the Temple being rent, as in section 105, but this section of the manuscript is so badly damaged that we cannot reconstruct it.

**101** As themes and images are repeated in Philip, they become more familiar and understandable. As we go on, we pick up the language of Philip, which is primarily concerned with body, soul, and spirit: the separation of the soul from the body, the return of the soul to unite with the spirit, and the forces that wish to prevent this.

**102** Those who are united in the bridal chamber are married, which is why they cannot be separated. The separation of the female from the male typifies the human condition. Making love within the bridal chamber represents the unification of the soul with the spirit.

**103** Just as breathing is a sign of humans and animals being physically alive, so the breath of the spirit gives spiritual life, and the absence of it is spiritual death. Since this section is concerned with soul and spirit, which are internal things, we are entitled to assume that the powers are also internal things. They are parts of our psychology that are only interested in the things of this world. Throughout the Gospel of Philip it is emphasized that the powers are powerless in the presence of the spirit.

Those who pray for Jerusalem [...] Jerusalem [...] those called the holy of holies [...] the veil was rent [...] the bridal chamber [...] ... except the image above. So, the veil was torn from top to bottom, because some from below had to ascend.[100]

69 The powers cannot see nor restrain those who are clothed in perfect light. One shall be clothed in light in the mystery of unity.[101]

70 If the female had not been separated from the male, she would not die with the male. His separation was the origin of death. For this, Christ came, so that he might correct the separation that has existed from the beginning, by uniting the two together. Now, a woman unites with her husband in the bridal chamber. Those who have coupled in the bridal chamber can no longer be separated. So, Eve separated from Adam because she did not unite with him in the bridal chamber.[102]

71 The soul of Adam came forth through a breath, whose companion is the Christ. The companion of his soul is the spirit. What was given to him was his mother. His soul was taken and replaced by the spirit. When he was united to it, the powers envied him because he was above them. They [...] spirit partner [...] bridal chamber.[103]

**104** When Jesus is baptized in the Gospel of Mark, a voice from heaven proclaims, "You are my son, the Beloved, with you I am well pleased" (Mark 1:11). It is in this sense that he was begotten by the father since he was adopted as a son at that moment. See note 28 for differing views of Eastern and Western Valentinianism on this.

**105** Rest refers to the day of rest, the sabbath. It is used repeatedly in Gnosticism and other parts of early Christianity, and is sometimes translated as repose. In the Gospel of Philip and elsewhere, it is synonymous with the spiritual level.

**106** *Adamah* means "earth" in biblical Hebrew, thus Adam is the earthly man, which explains his being born from the virgin earth. The Gospel of Philip has already established that the spirit is female and is a virgin.

**107** The two trees are the tree of life and the tree of knowledge of good and evil. Although the reason behind this is not clearly stated, the tree of knowledge of good and evil produces animals. The children of Adam who worship beasts are therefore the followers of pagan religion.

72 Jesus appeared by the Jordan in the fullness of the kingdom of heaven. The man born before all things was reborn. He was begotten, he was anointed, he was redeemed.104

73 It is appropriate to speak of a mystery: the father of all united with the virgin who came down to below and lit a fire for him on that day. He revealed the power of the great bridal chamber. It was for this that his body came to exist on that day. He came forth from the bridal chamber as one who had been with the bridegroom and bride. So Jesus established everything through these. It is right for each of the disciples to enter his rest.105

74 Adam came into being through two virgins— through the spirit and through the virgin earth. This is why Christ was born through a virgin, to rectify the fall which occurred in the beginning.106

75 Two trees grow in paradise. One bears animals, the others bears men. Adam ate from the tree which produced animals, and he begot animals. For this reason, the children of Adam worship beasts. The tree [...] fruit is [...] increased [...] ate the [...] fruit of the [...] bears men [...] 107

(continued on page 73)

**108** Judaism was unique among ancient religions because of its lack of idols and lack of visual depiction of its god. Christianity inherited something of this, although it adopted some of the pagan traditions of depicting gods, which eventually led to the great tradition of religious art. The philosophical question posed here may be asked of any aspect of any religion: Was it created by God or by humanity? Is it a way of developing the spirit, or simply a part of human culture? Philip puts a comical touch in at the end by suggesting that the pagan gods should worship humanity because humanity invented them.

**109** God worked for six days and then rested on the seventh, which leads to the contrast between work and rest used here.

**110** Why would free men work for slaves? Because the free would be able to release the slaves from their slavery. In Semitic idiom, the sons of the bridal chamber are the attendants of the bridegroom, while the sons of the marriage are the wedding guests.

**111** Going down into the water refers to baptism again. Unfortunately some of the most important words are missing from this passage.

God created man, but now men create God. This is how it is in the world—men make gods and worship their own creations. It would be more appropriate for the gods to worship men![108]

76 Someone's works depend on his powers. So his works are called his powers. Among his works are his children. They came into being through rest. Because of this, his power resides in his works, but his rest is apparent in his children. You will find that this even applies to the image. He does his works through his power, but begets his children through rest.[109]

77 In this world, slaves are made to work for free men. In the kingdom of heaven, the free will serve the slaves; the sons of the bridal chamber will serve the sons of the marriage. The sons of the bridal chamber have a single name: rest. Rest happens to them together, they will not need [...] contemplation of the image [...] things [...] glories.[110]

78 Those who go down into the water [...] ransom him [...] after he has gone out, in his name. For he said, "In this way we complete all righteousness."[111]

**112** The church father Epiphanius, in his typically negative way, writes of Valentinians, "They deny the resurrection of the dead, saying something mysterious and ridiculous, that it is not this body which rises, but another one rises from it, which they call 'spiritual.'"

**113** Since Joseph, and hence Jesus, is said to be a carpenter, there is plenty of scope for an ironic interpretation in which Joseph made the cross on which Jesus was crucified. Since the cross is made of wood, there are numerous parallels to be made between the cross and other trees. The cross is called a tree in a number of places, and crucifixion is being "hung from a tree." This saying goes further and points out that the tree of knowledge of good and evil killed Adam, just as the cross killed Jesus.

In the medieval Golden Legend and other traditions, Adam's son Seth (who is an initiate in some Gnostic writings and whose name was used to describe a whole branch of Gnosticism, "Sethianism") plants a branch from the tree of knowledge on Adam's tomb; the tree grows and eventually a bridge is made from it, Solomon having unsuccessfully tried to use it in the building of the Temple. This beam of wood is eventually used to construct the cross.

In the medieval version, the tree is a fig tree. Philip prefers an olive tree, as this gives a further connection to the chrism, the oil which was used for anointing, which was typically olive oil.

The third-century Pseudo-Clementine Recognitions also have this connection between the oil of anointing and the tree of life. It is worth quoting since it contains other terms that are typical of the Gospel of Philip: "Him first God anointed with oil which was taken from the wood of the tree of life: from that anointing therefore He is called Christ. Thence, moreover, He Himself also, according to the appointment of His Father, anoints with similar oil every one of the pious when they come to His kingdom, for their refreshment after their labors, as having got over the difficulties of the way; so that their light may shine, and being filled with the holy spirit, they may be endowed with immortality."

**79** Those who say that they will first die and then arise are mistaken. If they do not receive the resurrection first while they are alive, then they will receive nothing when they die. So also when speaking of baptism, it is said that baptism is a great thing, for those receiving it will live.[112]

**80** The apostle Philip said, Joseph the carpenter planted a garden full of trees because he needed wood for his craft. He made the cross from the trees that he had planted and his seed hung from what he had planted. The seed was Jesus and the plant was the cross. But the tree of life is in the middle of the garden. From the olive tree comes chrism and from chrism the resurrection.[113]

**114** In the physical world, eating means death, since whatever we eat must be killed in some way or another. But in the realm of truth, eating gives life.

**115** A clever and radical reworking of Genesis, here it is the dichotomy of "eat/do not eat" itself that constitutes the knowledge of good and evil. It was God who told Adam which of the trees he could eat from and which he could not, but paradoxically that in itself has become the knowledge of good and evil, and the beginning of the law. Paul also tells us in Romans 8 that the law (i.e., the Jewish ritual practices and restrictions) is the law of sin and death, but he does this in a somewhat ambiguous way. According to Paul, the Jewish law exists to show us that we cannot keep it, and this reveals our sin; the true law is the law of the spirit. It was Christianity's rejection of the practices of Jewish law that made it into a separate religion.

81 This world eats corpses—everything which is eaten in it dies. Truth eats life, so no one fed by the truth will die. Jesus came from within that place and he brought nourishment from there. And he gave life to those who wish it so that they might not die.[114]

82 God created a garden. Man [...] garden. There are [...] and [...] of God [...]

that garden is where it shall be said to me, "eat this or do not eat that, as you wish." The tree of knowledge is in the place where I will eat all things. That tree killed Adam, but here the tree of knowledge makes men live. The law was that tree. It has the power to give the knowledge of good and evil. It did not prevent him from evil nor preserve him for good, but it created death for those who have eaten it. For when he said, "eat this, do not eat that," it became the beginning of death.[115]

**116** Though it is literally an anointing with oil, the chrism ultimately refers to the process of becoming Christ.

**117** This is presented as a dominical saying, that is, a saying ascribed to Jesus. In Gnostic writings, there are a number of references to the laughter of Jesus. Jesus's laughter is notably absent in other traditions. In the Apocalypse of Peter, another of the texts found at Nag Hammadi, the following passage appears: "The Savior said to me, 'He whom you saw on the tree, glad and laughing, this is the living Jesus. But this one into whose hands and feet they drive the nails is his fleshly part, which is the substitute being put to shame, the one who came into being in his likeness. But look at him and me.'"

83 Christ is lord over baptism. For it is from chrism
that we are called Christians, not because of the
baptism. And he was called Christ because of the
chrism.116 For the father anointed the son and the
son anointed the apostles, and the apostles anointed
us. Whoever is anointed has everything—he has the
resurrection, the light, the cross, the holy spirit.
The father gave this to him in the bridal chamber
and he received it. The father was in the son and
the son in the father. This is the kingdom of heaven.

84 The Lord said it well: some attained the kingdom
of heaven laughing and rejoiced as they came out of
the world. And they came out [...] because [...]
a Christian [...]

And as soon as Jesus went down into the water, he
came forth lord of all because [...] a small thing
[...] but full of contempt for this [...] the kingdom
of heaven. If he despises [...] and scorns it as a small
thing, he will come out laughing.117 This is how it is
with the bread and the cup and the oil—but there
are others higher than these.

**118** One of the fundamental aspects of the Gnostic myth is the creation of the world by the demiurge, the inferior god, who is often called Yaldabaoth (see note 29). The Gospel of Philip doesn't focus on this to the extent that other Gnostic texts do. Philip prefers to focus on the positive aspects of being a son who can know the father, rather than on the negative aspects of being trapped in a material world created by the demiurge.

**119** Section 39 tells us that faith receives and love gives.

**120** In the ancient world, wine and water were commonly mixed when wine was drunk, which presumably suggested this imagery. That wine and water are a type of the blood suggests the crucifixion in John 19, when water and blood poured out of Jesus's side. It is interesting that it is not just wine that must be drunk to receive the perfect man, but wine and water, just as water and light are required if you want to see yourself. Maurice Nicoll, a student of Gurdjieff and Ouspensky, suggested that water represents truth and wine represents understanding.

**121** Living water is running water, not stagnant water, as in a river used for baptism. Also it is water that makes one spiritually alive. The metaphors in the Gospel of Philip are continually shifting, demanding a flexibility of understanding in the reader. In the previous saying, it is necessary to drink wine and water to receive the perfect man; here the body of the living water must put on the living man as if the latter is clothing. Though this is a bizarre image, it is easily understood within the context of Philip's metaphor. This is another example of taking off clothes, being naked, and then putting on better clothes (see note 35 above). A saying like this can have no meaning unless it is interpreted esoterically.

**85** The world came into being through a sin. For he who made it wanted to make it imperishable and immortal. He fell away and did not attain his ambition. For the world was not imperishable and immortal, nor was he who made the world. For things are not imperishable, only sons are, and no one can receive imperishability unless he is an offspring.[118] Yet he who cannot receive certainly cannot give.[119]

**86a** The cup of prayer contains wine and water, since it is established as a type of the blood over which they give thanks. And it is full of the holy spirit and it belongs to the complete and perfect man. Whenever we drink this, we receive the perfect man.[120]

**86b** The living water is a body. It is essential that we should be clothed by the living man. Because of this, someone comes down to the water and strips himself naked in order that he might be clothed by him.[121]

**122** Philip is fascinated by the idea of children resembling parents and the opportunities that this presents for spiritual metaphor. The lacunae prevent us from following the flow of meaning here.

**123** It is difficult to follow the development of thought here. The form of union in the eternal aeon is different to the union of the male and female, the strong and the weak in this world. The thought becomes lost in the difficulty of understanding exactly how the various elements of this passage relate to each other.

**124** A similar idea to the Gospel of Thomas 67 is expressed here. Thomas has, "Whoever knows everything but lacks himself, lacks a place within himself."

**87** A horse begets a horse, a human begets a human, a god begets a god. This is how it is with the bridegroom and the bride, they both come from the [...] A Jew [...] exists [...] and from Jews [...] Christians [...] this place is called [...] the chosen people of the [...] and the true man and the son of man and the seed of the son of man. This true people is renowned in the world: this is where the sons of the bridal chamber dwell.[122]

**88** In this world, union is between man and woman, where there is strength and weakness. But in the eternal aeon, the form of union is different. Although we refer to them by the same names, they are superior to every name and are superior to strength. For where there is strength, there are also those who are superior to strength. These are not separate things but are the same single thing. This is what will not be able to enter into hearts of flesh.[123]

**89** It is essential that those who possess everything should know themselves. Some certainly will not enjoy what they possess unless they know themselves. But those who have come to know themselves will enjoy it.[124]

**125** This idea of perfect light is very similar to the idea expressed in section 69.

**126** A somewhat different approach to the body is expressed here, reminding us once again that Philip is an anthology excerpted from other writings. For the most part in the Gospel of Philip, the body is disregarded in favor of the spirit. Yet here we are told that the holy man can purify his body. This hints at the ascetic practices that already existed in second-century Christianity and have persisted throughout the history of Christianity.

**127** *Pneuma* means both wind and spirit. The wind of the world brings winter and blows us away, but the wind of the spirit brings summer, which is the eternal realm of section 4.

**128** The notable Philip scholar Martha Lee Turner sees this as the beginning of the final section of the Gospel of Philip. She proposes that the last quarter of the text is taken from an early Valentinian document. Though the Gospel of Philip encourages us to find equivalences and parallels between its various passages, we should always keep in mind that it is an anthology of excerpts from other writings.

**129** This passage reverses Paul's notion that gnosis (knowledge) "puffs up" and instead interprets it as "building up." As Paul writes in 1 Corinthians, "Now concerning food offered to idols: we know that 'all of us possess knowledge.' Knowledge puffs up, but love builds up. If any one imagines that he knows something, he does not yet know as he ought to know. But if one loves God, one is known by him. Hence, as to the eating of food offered to idols, we know that 'an idol has no real existence,' and that 'there is no God but one'" (1 Cor. 8:1).

In his Stromata, Clement of Alexandria, the proto-orthodox church father who has some affinity to Gnosticism, states, "Now the Greek philosophy, as it were, purges the soul, and prepares it beforehand for the reception of faith, on which the Truth builds up the edifice of knowledge."

90 Not only will the perfect man not be able to be captured, but he cannot even be seen. For if they saw him they would seize him. In no other way can one be begotten of this grace unless one should put on the perfect light and become perfect light. Whoever has put it on will go in [...] This is the perfect light that we [...] imperfect. Only Jesus can know the destiny of that one.[125]

91 The holy man is entirely holy, down to his very body. If such a man receives bread he makes it holy, or the cup, or everything else he receives. How shall he not purify the body also?[126]

92 By perfecting the water of baptism, Jesus poured away death. Because of this, we indeed go down into the water, but we do not go down into death, so that we are not poured out onto the wind of the world. When the wind blows, winter comes; whenever the holy spirit blows, summer comes.[127]

93 Whoever knows the truth is free.[128] And whoever is free does not sin, for he who sins is the slave of sin. Truth is the mother, knowledge the father. Those who do not sin are called free in the world. As for those not given to sin, knowledge of the truth "builds them up" which is what the words "it makes them free" mean, and "it builds them up" as regards the whole place. But love builds up.[129]

(continued on page 87)

**130** This reminds me of the Sufi story where a suitor goes to the house of his Beloved. She asks who is there and he replies, "It is I." She tells him to go away because there is only room for one in the house. He later comes back and when she asks who is there, he replies, "It is thou." And he is let into the house.

**131** Fragrance represents a different state of matter than that represented by wine, more akin to spirit. Fragrance is invisible, can spread over a wide area, yet is definitely there. Wine has to be contained in a cup, and can be seen. The fragrance may also come from oil.

Philo of Alexandria compares the presence of wise men to fragrances: "For, as those spices which are set on fire fill all persons near them with their fragrance, so in the same manner do all those persons who are neighbors of and contiguous to the wise men catch some of the exhalations which reach to a distance from him, and so become improved in their characters."

**132** The images of wine and fragrance are transformed into an exegesis of the story of the Good Samaritan.

He who is free because of knowledge is a slave because of love, for the sake of those who have not yet received the freedom of knowledge. Knowledge makes them able to be free. Love never calls something its own [...] It never says, this is mine and that is yours, but it says that all this is yours.[130]

94 Spiritual love is wine with fragrance. All those who are anointed with it enjoy it. While those who are anointed remain, those who stand beside them also enjoy it. But if those who are anointed with the chrism withdraw and depart, those who are not anointed stand by and remain in their own scent.[131] The Samaritan gave nothing but wine and oil to the wounded man—and it healed the wounds because love heals a multitude of sins.[132]

**133** The folk belief that the children born of a woman who while making love sees or imagines another man or some other image will resemble the man or image rather than the biological father turns out to be extraordinarily widespread. Evidence for this belief extends from Aristotle and Empedocles, who discuss children who do not resemble their parents, to the Bible and rabbinical writings, to the *Mahabharata,* and even to modern European writers such as Goethe.

In Genesis, Jacob makes sure that his sheep are staring at striped, spotted, and patched rods while they breed so that their lambs will also have stripes, spots, or patches. Soran, whose writings were late second century, roughly contemporary with the Gospel of Philip, wrote that women who saw monkeys while they made love gave birth to children who resembled monkeys and that the deformed king of the Cyprians made his wife look at beautiful statues during sex, so that she gave birth to beautiful children who resembled the statues rather than him. This belief also occurs in rabbinical literature: "Our Rabbis said: When a woman is with her husband and is engaged in intercourse with him, and at the same time her heart is with another man whom she has seen on the road, there is no greater adultery than this; for it is said, 'The wife commits adultery, taking strangers while under her husband'" (Ezekiel 16:32). This idea finds its literary culmination in Goethe's novel *Elective Affinities,* in which a husband and wife each imagine their lovers while they have intercourse and the resulting child looks like a cross between their two lovers rather than themselves.

The rabbinical text is very close to Philip, yet Philip differs from all other accounts of this tradition in that, even here, the point is being used metaphorically. On the other hand, scholar April DeConick thinks that this is evidence of actual sexual practice among Valentinians, in that they would have encouraged each other to think of God during intercourse, rather than the things of this world.

95 The children born of a woman will resemble the man whom she loves. If it is her husband whom she loves, then her husband will love her; if it is an adulterer then they will resemble the adulterer. Often, if a woman sleeps with her husband out of necessity, yet her heart is with the adulterer, and she unites with him, and bears children, then the one to whom she gives birth will resemble the adulterer. Then you who live with the son of god, do not love the world; rather, love the Lord, so that those whom you beget will not be made to resemble the world but will be made to resemble the Lord.[133]

**134** In the ancient world, the brutish Minotaur was an example of a mixed union. This saying leaves us in no doubt that sex is used as metaphor.

**135** That the free man can sell himself back into slavery suggests that a pneumatic can cease being a pneumatic at any time.

96 Humans unite with humans; horses unite with horses; the ass with the ass. Each species unite with their fellow species. In this way, the spirit unites with the spirit, the Word with the Word, and light unites with light. If you become human then a human will love you. If you become a spirit then the spirit will unite with you. If you become Word, then the Word will unite with you. If you become light, it is light which will couple with you. If you become one of those from above, it is those from above who will rest on you. If you become horse or ass or bull or dog or sheep, or any other animal from outside or from below, then neither mankind nor the spirit, nor the Word, nor the light, nor those from above, nor those within will be able to love you. Neither those from above, nor those from within, will be able to rest within you, and they will have no part in you.[134]

97 He who is an unwilling slave is able to become free. He who has become free as a gift of his master, and has sold himself back into slavery will no longer be able to be free.[135]

**136** Although this is an intriguing identification of the four elements with Paul's faith, hope, and love, along with knowledge, or gnosis, these cannot really be used to interpret earth or water or wind or light in the rest of the Gospel of Philip.

**137** The beatitude unfortunately breaks off. The German Philip expert H. M. Schenke suggested that it might be reconstructed, "Blessed is he because he has not grieved any souls!"

**138** The passages in this last quarter of the Gospel of Philip tend to be longer than those in the earlier part. This reflects the nature of the source used by Philip. This source seems to be rather more similar to the Gospel of Truth, the only extended piece of writing that might be ascribed to Valentinus. These passages are more internally consistent with each other, yet still reflect the overall interests of the Gospel of Philip.

98 The agriculture of the world results from four things—a harvest is gathered into the barn through earth and water and wind and light. Cultivation by God is also through four things: faith, hope, love, and knowledge. Earth is our faith, in which we take root; water is hope through which we are nourished; wind is love through which we grow; and light is gnosis through which we ripen.[136]

99 Blessed is he who has not caused a soul [...][137]

That man is Jesus Christ. He came to the entire place and did not burden anyone. So, blessed is he who is like this: he is a perfect man. For the world tells us that this kind is hard to define. Who of us can achieve such a great thing? How will he give rest to everyone? For one must not cause distress to anyone, whether great or small, believer or unbeliever. Then one must provide rest for those who rest in what is good. Some people find advantage in giving rest to those who have fared well in life. He who does good cannot give rest to such people, for he who is good does not just seize on whatever he likes. He is unable to cause distress, however, for he does not aggrieve them. But he who is perfect sometimes aggrieves them—not that he is thus, but rather it is their own evil that causes them grief. He who possesses perfection bestows joy on the good—yet some people grieve badly at this.[138]

**139** Here we have a parable followed by an explanation of it. Giving different foods to different kinds of creatures and humans corresponds to giving different kinds of teaching to different kinds of disciples. Perhaps this is an extended version of Paul's comments in 1 Corinthians 3:2 about feeding his followers milk, not solid food. Paul tells his followers in the church in Corinth that they are not ready for solid food (or "strong meat" in the pungent translation of the King James Version) because they are still of the flesh.

**100** The master of a household obtained everything, whether it was son or slave or dog or cattle or pig, whether wheat or barley or straw or hay or [...] or meat and acorn. He was wise and knew what food was right for each of them. He served the sons bread, but he served the slaves [...] and grain. He fed barley to the cattle, with straw and hay, to the dogs he threw bones, and to the pigs acorns and slops.

So it is with the disciples of God. If they are wise they can discriminate about discipleship. Bodily forms will not deceive him, but he will look at the condition of the soul in each one in order to speak with him. In the world there are many animals made in the form of man—he recognizes these, so that to the pigs he will throw acorns, yet to the cattle he will throw barley with straw and hay, and to the dogs he will throw bones, to the slaves he will give elementary food. To sons he will give the perfect food.[139]

**140** The son of man was a title given to Jesus, though it was also used in other ways, for instance as an indirect way of referring to oneself. In this passage, the "son of man" is specifically defined as being the Lord. The difference between creating and begetting is then compared to the difference between the revealed and the hidden, particularly since begetting, which is the result of sexual intercourse, is done in secret. Curiously, according to this passage, a child is not begotten but created, since a child is a creature.

**141** Much of the same ground is covered here as in section 27 (see note 47).

**101** There is the son of man and there is the son of the son of man. The son of man is the Lord and the son of the son of man is he who creates through the son of man. The son of man received from God the ability to create as well as to beget. That which is created is a creature, that which is begotten is a son.**140** A creature cannot beget. A begotten one can also create. Yet it is said that a creature begets, but a child is a creature. So their offspring are not begotten but created. He who creates works openly and is himself revealed. He who begets does so in secret and is himself hidden since […] image. And he who creates does so openly, but he who begets, begets secretly and is hidden […] image. He who creates does so visibly, while he who begets bears offspring in secret.**141**

**142** These are quite specific directions on how to behave in the bridal chamber. It is only appropriate for certain people to know what goes on in the bridal chamber. These include the bridegroom's friend, who in the Gospel of John is John the Baptist. The sons of the bridal chamber is a Semitic idiom for the companions of the bridegroom. See, for example, Matthew 9:15 and its parallels in Mark and Luke, "And Jesus said unto them, Can the children of the bridechamber mourn, as long as the bridegroom is with them? But the days will come, when the bridegroom shall be taken from them, and then shall they fast."

In essence, section 102 is concerned with spiritual secrecy. Only the person who is in the bridal chamber can understand what it means.

**143** An extensive amount of metaphorical interpretation surrounded the physical practice of circumcision. Christians didn't need to be circumcised, and so they were interested only in the spiritual implications of the image of circumcision. Jews approached this from a slightly different point of view: since the mere circumcision of the penis could hardly be considered sufficient for God, a true circumcision involved the internal aspects of a person. Paul, who was a Jew, tells us that, "For he is not a real Jew who is one outwardly, nor is true circumcision something external and physical. He is a Jew who is one inwardly, and real circumcision is a matter of the heart, spiritual and not literal. His praise is not from men but from God" (Rom. 2:28–29). The prophets of the Hebrew Bible were often concerned with the circumcision of the heart. Philo of Alexandria develops this: "Thirdly, there is the resemblance of the part that is circumcised to the heart; for both parts are prepared for the sake of generation; for the breath contained within the heart is generative of thoughts, and the generative organ itself is productive of living beings." And also, "I see here a twofold circumcision, one of the male creature and the other of the flesh; that which is of the flesh takes place in the genitals, but that which is of the male creature takes place, as it seems to me, in respect to his thoughts. Since that which is, properly speaking, masculine in us is the intellect, the superfluous

*(continued on page 100)*

**102** No one can know when a man and woman unite with each other, except themselves. For marriage in the world is a mystery for those who have married. If the defiled marriage is hidden, how much more is the undefiled marriage a true mystery. It is not fleshly but holy; it does not belong to desire but to the will. It does not belong to the darkness and the night, but to the day and the light. If a marriage is revealed it becomes prostitution. And the bride has made a whore of herself not only if she receives the seed of another man, but if she leaves the chamber and is seen. She may only reveal herself to the father and the mother, and to the friend of the bridegroom, and the sons of the bridal chamber. These are allowed to enter each day into the bridal chamber. Yet for the others, let them yearn to hear her voice and enjoy her fragrance and let them feed like dogs from the crumbs that fall from the table. Bridegrooms and brides belong to the bridal chamber. No one can see the bridegroom with the bride unless he has become one of these.[142]

**103** When Abraham [...] to behold what he was to behold, he circumcised the flesh of the foreskin, teaching us that it is proper to destroy the flesh.[143]

shoots of which it is necessary to prune away and to cast off, so that it, becoming clean and pure from all wickedness and vile, may worship God as his priest. This therefore is what is designated by the second circumcision, where God says by an express law, 'Circumcise the hardness of your heart,' that is to say, your hard and rebellious thoughts and ambition, which when they are cut away and removed from you, your most important part will be rendered free."

The Gospel of Thomas 53 praises the true circumcision in spirit. The Odes of Solomon makes beautiful use of circumcision in its poetry: "My heart was pruned and its flower appeared, then grace sprang up in it, and my heart produced fruits for the Lord. For the Most High circumcised me by His holy spirit, then He uncovered my inward being towards Him, and filled me with His love. And His circumcising became my salvation, and I ran in the Way, in His peace, in the way of truth."

The Gospel of Philip connects circumcision with the mortality of the flesh.

**144** Perhaps the comparison with bowels is significant in representing the deepest part of the body. The rest of this passage is an extended commentary on John the Baptist's statement that "already the axe is laid at the root of the tree."

104 As long as the inner parts are hidden, most things in the world can stand upright and live. If they are revealed, they die, as is the case with the visible aspects of human beings: as long as the bowels of a man are hidden, the man is alive; when his bowels are revealed and come out of him, the man shall die.[144] So also with a tree: it sprouts and grows while its root is hidden, but if its root is revealed, the tree withers. Thus it is with everything in the world, not only with the revealed but also with the hidden. For as long as the root of evil is hidden, it is strong. But when it is recognized it has perished, and as soon as it is revealed it ceases to exist. That is why the Word says, "already the axe is laid at the root of the trees."

It will not merely chop off, for that which is chopped off sprouts again. Rather the axe digs down until it finds the root. Jesus pulled up the root of the entire place, yet others did so only partially.

Let each of us dig down for the root of evil that is within us and root it up from our hearts. It will be uprooted when it is recognized. But if we are ignorant of it, it bears its fruits within our hearts.

(continued on page 103)

145 Knowledge should be understood as gnosis and ignorance as the lack of gnosis. Philip again confounds our analytical minds by switching rapidly between the metaphors of knowledge and ignorance, truth and error, freedom and slavery. The process of revealing the truth also reveals the evil and error that is deep in our hearts.

It masters us and we are its slaves. It takes us captives, makes us do what we do not wish to do, and not do what we want to do. It is powerful because we have not recognized it. As long as it exists it is active.

Ignorance is the mother of all evils. Lack of knowledge leads to death. For those who exist from lack of knowledge neither were, nor are, nor will be [...] will become perfect when all the truth is revealed. For truth is like ignorance, while it is hidden it rests within itself, but when it is revealed and it is recognized, it is glorified inasmuch as it overpowers ignorance and error. It gives freedom. The Word says, "If you shall know the truth, the truth will set you free." Ignorance is slavery, knowledge is freedom. If we recognize the truth, we shall find the fruits of truth within our hearts. By uniting with it we shall receive our fulfillment.[145]

146 The language of this passage is quite apocalyptic, with the building being destroyed and water flooding out. But the intention is clearly not to predict any forthcoming events in the external world, since the Temple had already been destroyed and Jerusalem razed to the ground by the time that the Gospel of Philip had been compiled. Rather, the passage refers to internal truth, expressed in "types and images."

**105** At present we have the revealed things of creation. We say that they are what is strong and glorious, while hidden things are weak and contemptible. But the revealed things of truth are not like this: they are weak and despised, while the hidden things are strong and noble. The mysteries of truth are revealed in type and image. But the bridal chamber is hidden—it is the holy within the holy. The veil at first concealed how God controlled creation, but when the veil is rent and what is inside is revealed, then this building will be left desolate, or will rather be destroyed. And all divinity will flee from here, but not into the holy of holies, for it will not be able to unite with the unblended light of the flawless fullness. Rather, it will be under the wings and the arms of the cross. This ark will be salvation when the flood of water surges over them.[146]

(*continued on page* 107)

**147** The veil that separates the holy of holies, or the bridal chamber, from the outside is torn from the top all the way to the bottom. This symbolizes a two way communication between what is within the holy of holies and what is outside of it, by which divinity can contact us and we can contact divinity.

**148** Many connections are made between the bridal chamber and the Temple. The Jerusalem Temple was destroyed in 70 CE, but later Jewish and Christian texts still make extensive reference to it, and the very fact of its physical demise encouraged its use as a spiritual metaphor. This description of the Temple is reminiscent of the Epistle to the Hebrews: "For a tent was prepared, the outer one, in which were the lampstand and the table and the bread of the Presence; it is called the Holy Place. Behind the second curtain stood a tent called the Holy of Holies" (Hebrews 9:4). In the canonical gospels, the veil of the Temple is torn in two just as Jesus dies. The Gospel of Philip refers explicitly to this and interprets it positively, since this rending of the veil allows us to enter into truth.

If some belong to the order of the priesthood, they shall be allowed to enter within the veil with the high priest. This is why the veil was not only rent at the top, since it would have only been opened to those from above, nor was it rent at the bottom since it would have been revealed only to those from below. Rather, it was torn from the top to the bottom.[147] Those who are above opened to us the things that are below, so that we may enter into the secret of the truth; this truly is what is glorious and strong. Yet we shall enter in by means of types and other weak things. They are humble in the presence of perfect glory. There is a glory above glory and a power above power. Thus the perfect things have opened to us, along with the hidden things of truth. The holies of holies are revealed and the bedchamber has invited us in.[148]

**149**　This quotation is from the Gospel of Matthew 15:13. Ignatius's letter to the Trallians says, "Avoid therefore the evil branches that produce deadly fruit, of which if any man taste he dieth forthwith. These, therefore, are not the planting of the Father."

**106** As long as the seed of the holy spirit is hidden, evil is powerless, but has not been removed and they are enslaved to evil. But when it is revealed, the perfect light will pour on everyone and all who are within it shall receive the chrism. Then the slaves will be freed and the captives ransomed. "Every plant which my father in heaven has not planted shall be rooted up."[149] Those who are separated shall be united and shall become full.

150 There is no particular significance in this passage being the last section of the Gospel of Philip, but it does contain a reprise of some of
the major themes and images of the text—light and darkness, day and
night, the aeon and the world, truth and images, and the bridal chamber. The fire of lovemaking, which takes place at night and burns itself
out, is contrasted with the union of spiritual marriage, which takes
place in the day and in the light. The title "The Gospel of Philip" is
given at the end of the text as a colophon.

**107** Everyone who enters the bridal chamber will kindle the light. For [...] just as the marriages which are revealed occur at night, that fire burns only at night and is put out. But the mysteries of this marriage are consummated in the day and in the light, and that day does not set, nor does its light.

If anyone becomes a son of the bridal chamber, he will receive the light. If he does not receive it in this place he will not be able to receive it in the other place. He who will receive this light cannot be seen, nor can he be captured. No one can disturb such a one even while he dwells in the world. Moreover, when he leaves the world, he has already received truth in the images. The world has become the aeon and the aeon is fullness for him. Thus it is revealed to him alone—not hidden in darkness or night, but hidden in a perfect day and a holy light.[150]

THE GOSPEL OF PHILIP

# Notes ☐

## Introduction

1. See Stevan Davies, *The Gospel of Thomas and Christian Wisdom* (Oregon House, Calif.: Bardic Press, 2005).

2. Michael Williams, *Rethinking "Gnosticism": An Argument for Dismantling a Dubious Category* (Princeton: Princeton University Press, 1999).

3. In an earlier book I provided some outlines for an interpretation of the Gospel of Thomas. See Andrew Phillip Smith, *The Gospel of Thomas: A New Version Based on Its Inner Meaning* (Oregon House, Calif.: Ulysses Books, 2002).

4. Elaine Pagels, *Adam, Eve, and the Serpent* (New York: Random House, 1988), 4.

5. In *The Gospel of Thomas: A New Version Based on Its Inner Meaning,* I provided the basis for an interpretation of Thomas along these lines.

6. Irenaeus, *Against Heresies,* in *The Ante-Nicene Fathers,* ed. Alexander Roberts and James Donaldson (Grand Rapids, Mich.: Eerdmans, 1981), I.13.2.

## Annotations

8. Philo of Alexandria, *Special Laws,* in *The Works of Philo,* trans. C. D. Yonge (Peabody, Mass.: Hendrickson, 1993), IV.179.

13. Elaine Pagels, *The Origin of Satan* (New York: Random House, 1995), 171.

24. Valentinus frag. H, in Bentley Layton, *The Gnostic Scriptures,* (New York: Doubleday, 1995).

27. "The Reality of the Rulers," in Bentley Layton, *The Gnostic Scriptures,* 72.

33. Origen, "Contra Celsum," cited in *Resurrection: New Testament Witness and Contemporary Reflection,* Pheme Perkins (New York: Doubleday, 1984), 73.

35. R. McL. Wilson, *The Gospel of Philip* (New York: Harper & Row, 1962), 89.

39. Wesley Isenberg, trans., "The Gospel of Philip," in *The Nag Hammadi Library in English,* ed. James Robinson, rev. ed. (San Francisco: Harper & Row, 1988).

41. Bentley Layton, *The Gnostic Scriptures* (New York: Doubleday, 1995).

44. H. V. Morton, *In the Steps of the Master* (London: Rich & Cowan, 1934), 154–55.

47. Stephen Emmel, trans., "Dialogue of the Savior," in *The Nag Hammadi Library in English,* 252.

51. Harold W. Attridge and Dieter Muller, trans., "The Tripartite Tractate," in *The Nag Hammadi Library in English,* 64.

52. Epiphanius, *Panarion/Against Heresies,* in *The Ante-Nicene Fathers,* 78.8.

66. Irenaeus, *Against Heresies,* in *The Ante-Nicene Fathers,* 1.23.3.

67. Ibid., 6.2.

72. J. H. Charlesworth, trans., "Odes of Solomon," in *The Old Testament Pseudepigrapha,* vol. 2, (New York: Doubleday, 1985), verse 35.

73. Oscar Cullman and Robert McL. Wilson, trans., "The Infancy Gospel of Thomas," in *New Testament Apocrypha,* vol. 1, *Gospels and Related Writings,* ed. R. McL. Wilson (Louisville, Ky.: John Knox Press, 1991), 453.

77. Charles W. Hedrick, trans., "The Second Apocalypse of James," in *The Nag Hammadi Library in English,* 274.

78. Irenaeus, *Apostolic Preaching 43,* in *The Ante-Nicene Fathers.*

88. "Acts of Philip," in M. R. James, ed., *The Apocryphal New Testament,* (Oxford: Oxford University Press, 1955), 450; Macrobius quoted in Timothy Freke and Peter Gandy, *The Jesus Mysteries: Was the "Original Jesus" a Pagan God?* (New York: Harmony Books, 1999), 112.

95. Elaine Pagels, *Adam, Eve, and the Serpent* (New York: Random House, 1988), 68.

96. Stephen MacKenna, trans., "Porphyry: On the Life of Plotinus and the Arrangement of His Work," in *The Enneads* (New York: Penguin Classics, 1991).

112. Epiphanius, *Panarion,* in *The Ante-Nicene Fathers,* 31, 7, 6, 7, 10.

113. *Clementine Recognitions,* in *The Ante-Nicene Fathers,* 1.45.

120. Maurice Nicoll, *The New Man* (London: Stuart and Richards, 1950).

128. Martha Lee Turner, *The Gospel According to Philip: The Sources and Coherence of an Early Christian Collection,* Nag Hammadi and Manichean Studies 38 (Leiden: Brill, 1996).

129. Clement of Alexandria, *Stromata,* in *The Ante-Nicene Fathers,* VII.104.5ff.

131. Philo, "On Dreams," in *The Works of Philo,* I.178.

133. Wendy Doniger and Gregory Spinner, "Misconceptions: Female Imaginations and Male Fantasies in Parental Imprinting," *Daedalus* 127 (Winter 1998): 97–130.

143. Philo, *Special Laws,* in *The Works of Philo,* 1.6; Philo, *Questions and Answers on Genesis,* in *The Works of Philo,* III.46; "Odes of Solomon," in *The Old Testament Pseudepigrapha,* 11:1–3.

149. *Ignatius' Letter to the Trallians,* in *The Ante-Nicene Fathers,* 11:1.

# Suggestions for Further Reading ☐

Barnstone, Willis, and Martin Meyer, eds. *The Gnostic Bible.* Boston: Shambhala, 2003.

Brown, Paterson Limb. "The Gospel of Philip," www.metalog.org/files/philip.html.

Davies, Stevan. *The Gospel of Thomas and Christian Wisdom.* Oregon House, Calif.: Bardic Press, 2005.

———, trans. and ann. *The Gospel of Thomas: Annotated and Explained.* Woodstock, Vt.: SkyLight Paths, 2002.

———, trans. and ann. *The Secret Book of John: The Gnostic Gospel—Annotated and Explained.* Woodstock, Vt.: SkyLight Paths, 2005.

De Conick, A. D. "The Great Mystery of Marriage: Sex and Conception in Ancient Valentinian Traditions." *Vigiliae Christianae* 57, no. 3 (2003): 307–42.

Ehrman, Bart. *Lost Scriptures: Books That Did Not Make It into the New Testament.* New York: Oxford University Press, 2003.

Freke, Timothy, and Peter Gandy. *The Jesus Mysteries: Was the "Original Jesus" a Pagan God?* New York: Harmony Books, 1999.

Isenberg, Wesley, trans. *The Nag Hammadi Library in English.* Edited by James Robinson. Rev. ed. San Francisco: Harper & Row, 1988.

James, M. R., ed., *The Apocryphal New Testament.* Oxford: Oxford University Press, 1955.

Layton, Bentley. *The Gnostic Scriptures: A New Translation with Annotations and Introductions.* Garden City, N.Y.: Doubleday, 1995.

———, ed. *Nag Hammadi Codex II, 2–7.* Vol. 1. Leiden: Brill, 1989.

Leloup, Jean-Yves. *The Gospel of Philip: Jesus, Mary Magdalene, and the Gnosis of Sacred Union.* Rochester, Vt.: Inner Traditions, 2004.

Pagels, Elaine. *Adam, Eve, and the Serpent.* New York: Random House, 1988.

———. *The Gnostic Paul: Gnostic Exegesis of the Pauline Letters.* Philadelphia: Trinity Press, 1992.

———. *The Origin of Satan.* New York: Random House, 1995.

Shapiro, Rami, trans. and ann. *The Divine Feminine in Biblical Wisdom Literature: Selections Annotated and Explained.* Woodstock, Vt.: SkyLight Paths, 2005.

Smith, Andrew Phillip. *The Gospel of Thomas: A New Version Based on Its Inner Meaning.* Oregon House, Calif.: Ulysses Books, 2002.

Turner, John D., and Anne McGuire, eds. *The Nag Hammadi Library after Fifty Years: Proceedings of the 1995 Society of Biblical Literature Commemoration,* Nag Hammadi and Manichaean Studies 44. Leiden: Brill, 1996. See articles by Martha Lee Turner, "On the Coherence of the Gospel According to Philip," 223–50; Einer Thomassen, "How Valentinian Is the Gospel of Philip?" 251–79; Elaine Pagels, "Ritual in the Gospel of Philip," 280–91.

Turner, Martha Lee. *The Gospel According to Philip: The Sources and Coherence of an Early Christian Collection*, Nag Hammadi and Manichaean Studies 38. Leiden: Brill, 1996.

Williams, Michael. *Rethinking "Gnosticism": An Argument for Dismantling a Dubious Category.* Princeton: Princeton University Press, 1999.

Wilson, R. McL. *The Gospel of Philip.* New York: Harper & Row, 1962.

———, ed. *New Testament Apocrypha.* Vol. 1, *Gospels and Related Writings.* Louisville, Ky.: John Knox Press, 1991.

## Global Spiritual Perspectives

**Spiritual Perspectives on America's Role as Superpower**
*by the Editors at SkyLight Paths*
Are we the world's good neighbor or a global bully? Explores broader issues surrounding the use of American power around the world, including in Iraq and the Middle East. From a spiritual perspective, what are America's responsibilities as the only remaining superpower? Contributors:

**Dr. Beatrice Bruteau • Rev. Dr. Joan Brown Campbell • Tony Campolo • Rev. Forrest Church • Lama Surya Das • Matthew Fox • Kabir Helminski • Thich Nhat Hanh • Eboo Patel • Abbot M. Basil Pennington, ocso • Dennis Prager • Rosemary Radford Ruether • Wayne Teasdale • Rev. William McD. Tully • Rabbi Arthur Waskow • John Wilson**
5½ x 8½, 256 pp, Quality PB, ISBN 1-893361-81-0 **$16.95**

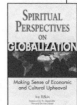

**Spiritual Perspectives on Globalization, 2nd Edition**
Making Sense of Economic and Cultural Upheaval
*by Ira Rifkin; Foreword by Dr. David Little, Harvard Divinity School*
What is globalization? What are spiritually minded people saying and doing about it? This lucid introduction surveys the religious landscape, explaining in clear and nonjudgmental language the beliefs that motivate spiritual leaders, activists, theologians, academics, and others involved on all sides of the issue. This edition includes a new Afterword and Discussion Guide designed for group use.
5½ x 8½, 256 pp, Quality PB, ISBN 1-59473-045-8 **$16.99**

## Hinduism / Vedanta

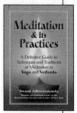

**Meditation & Its Practices:** A Definitive Guide to Techniques and Traditions of Meditation in Yoga and Vedanta
*by Swami Adiswarananda*
The complete sourcebook for exploring Hinduism's two most time-honored traditions of meditation. Drawing on both classic and contemporary sources, this comprehensive sourcebook outlines the scientific, psychological, and spiritual elements of Yoga and Vedanta meditation.
6 x 9, 504 pp, HC, ISBN 1-893361-83-7 **$34.95**

**Sri Sarada Devi:** Her Teachings and Conversations
*Translated and with Notes by Swami Nikhilananda*
*Edited and with an Introduction by Swami Adiswarananda*
Brings to life the Holy Mother's teachings on human affliction, self-control, and peace in ways both personal and profound, and illuminates her role as the power, scripture, joy, and guiding spirit of the Ramakrishna Order.
6 x 9, 288 pp, HC, ISBN 1-59473-070-9 **$29.99**

**The Vedanta Way to Peace and Happiness**
*by Swami Adiswarananda*
Using language that is accessible to people of all faiths and backgrounds, this book introduces the timeless teachings of Vedanta—divinity of the individual soul, unity of all existence, and oneness with the Divine—ancient wisdom as relevant to human happiness today as it was thousands of years ago.
6 x 9, 240 pp, HC, ISBN 1-59473-034-2 **$29.99**

*Or phone, fax, mail or e-mail to:* **SKYLIGHT PATHS** Publishing
Sunset Farm Offices, Route 4 • P.O. Box 237 • Woodstock, Vermont 05091
Tel: (802) 457-4000 • Fax: (802) 457-4004 • www.skylightpaths.com
*Credit card orders:* **(800) 962-4544** (8:30AM–5:30PM ET Monday–Friday)
*Generous discounts on quantity orders. SATISFACTION GUARANTEED. Prices subject to change.*

# Children's Spirituality

## Because Nothing Looks Like God
by Lawrence and Karen Kushner; Full-color illus. by Dawn W. Majewski
Real-life examples of happiness and sadness—from goodnight stories, to the hope and fear felt the first time at bat, to the closing moments of life—introduce children to the possibilities of spiritual life.
11 x 8½, 32 pp, HC, Full-color illus., ISBN 1-58023-092-X **$16.95**

*For ages 4 & up (a Jewish Lights book)*

Also available:

**Teacher's Guide,** 8½ x 11, 22 pp, PB, ISBN 1-58023-140-3 **$6.95** *For ages 5–8*

## Becoming Me: A Story of Creation
by Martin Boroson; Full-color illus. by Christopher Gilvan-Cartwright
Told in the personal "voice" of the Creator, here is a story about creation and relationship that is about each one of us.
8 x 10, 32 pp, Full-color illus., HC, ISBN 1-893361-11-X **$16.95** *For ages 4 & up*

## But God Remembered: Stories of Women from Creation to the Promised Land   by Sandy Eisenberg Sasso; Full-color illus. by Bethanne Andersen
A fascinating collection of four different stories of women only briefly mentioned in biblical tradition and religious texts; all teach important values through their actions and faith.   9 x 12, 32 pp, HC, Full-color illus., ISBN 1-879045-43-5 **$16.95**
*For ages 8 & up (a Jewish Lights book)*

## Cain & Abel: Finding the Fruits of Peace
by Sandy Eisenberg Sasso; Full-color illus. by Joani Keller Rothenberg
A sensitive recasting of the ancient tale shows we have the power to deal with anger in positive ways. Provides questions for kids and adults to explore together. "Editor's Choice"—American Library Association's *Booklist*
9 x 12, 32 pp, HC, Full-color illus., ISBN 1-58023-123-3 **$16.95** *For ages 5 & up (a Jewish Lights book)*

## Does God Hear My Prayer?
by August Gold; Full-color photo illus. by Diane Hardy Waller
This colorful book introduces preschoolers as well as young readers to prayer and how prayer can help them express their own fears, wants, sadness, surprise, and joy.   10 x 8½, 32 pp, Quality PB, Full-color photo illus., ISBN 1-59473-102-0 **$8.99**

## The 11th Commandment: Wisdom from Our Children
by The Children of America
"If there were an Eleventh Commandment, what would it be?" Children of many religious denominations across America answer this question—in their own drawings and words. "A rare book of spiritual celebration for all people, of all ages, for all time." —*Bookviews*
8 x 10, 48 pp, HC, Full-color illus., ISBN 1-879045-46-X **$16.95** *For ages 4 & up (a Jewish Lights book)*

## For Heaven's Sake
by Sandy Eisenberg Sasso; Full-color illus. by Kathryn Kunz Finney
Everyone talked about heaven: "Thank heavens." "Heaven forbid." "For heaven's sake, Isaiah." But no one would say what heaven was or how to find it. So Isaiah decides to find out, by seeking answers from many different people.
9 x 12, 32 pp, HC, Full-color illus., ISBN 1-58023-054-7 **$16.95** *For ages 4 & up (a Jewish Lights book)*

## God in Between
by Sandy Eisenberg Sasso; Full-color illus. by Sally Sweetland
If you wanted to find God, where would you look? A magical, mythical tale that teaches that God can be found where we are: within all of us and the relationships between us.   9 x 12, 32 pp, HC, Full-color illus., ISBN 1-879045-86-9 **$16.95**
*For ages 4 & up (a Jewish Lights book)*

# Spiritual Biography—SkyLight Lives

SkyLight Lives reintroduces the lives and works of key spiritual figures of our time—people who by their teaching or example have challenged our assumptions about spirituality and have caused us to look at it in new ways.

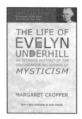   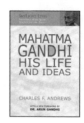

## The Life of Evelyn Underhill
### An Intimate Portrait of the Groundbreaking Author of *Mysticism*
*by Margaret Cropper; Foreword by Dana Greene*
Evelyn Underhill was a passionate writer and teacher who wrote elegantly on mysticism, worship, and devotional life. This is the story of how she made her way toward spiritual maturity, from her early days of agnosticism to the years when her influence was felt throughout the world.
6 x 9, 288 pp, 5 b/w photos, Quality PB, ISBN 1-893361-70-5 **$18.95**

## Mahatma Gandhi: His Life and Ideas
*by Charles F. Andrews; Foreword by Dr. Arun Gandhi*
Examines from a contemporary Christian activist's point of view the religious ideas and political dynamics that influenced the birth of the peaceful resistance movement, the primary tool that Gandhi and the people of his homeland would use to gain India its freedom from British rule.
6 x 9, 336 pp, 5 b/w photos, Quality PB, ISBN 1-893361-89-6 **$18.95**

## Simone Weil: A Modern Pilgrimage
*by Robert Coles*
The extraordinary life of the spiritual philosopher who's been called both saint and madwoman. Robert Coles' intriguing study of Weil is an insightful portrait of the beloved and controversial thinker whose life and writings influenced many (from T. S. Eliot to Adrienne Rich to Albert Camus), and continue to inspire seekers everywhere.
6 x 9, 208 pp, Quality PB, ISBN 1-893361-34-9 **$16.95**

## Zen Effects: The Life of Alan Watts
*by Monica Furlong*
Through his widely popular books and lectures, Alan Watts (1915–1973) did more to introduce Eastern philosophy and religion to Western minds than any figure before or since. Here is the first and only full-length biography of one of the most charismatic spiritual leaders of the twentieth century.
6 x 9, 264 pp, Quality PB, ISBN 1-893361-32-2 **$16.95**

# More Spiritual Biography

**Bede Griffiths:** An Introduction to His Interspiritual Thought
*by Wayne Teasdale* 6 x 9, 288 pp, Quality PB, ISBN 1-893361-77-2 **$18.95**

**Inspired Lives:** Exploring the Role of Faith and Spirituality in the Lives of Extraordinary People
*by Joanna Laufer and Kenneth S. Lewis* 6 x 9, 256 pp, Quality PB, ISBN 1-893361-33-0 **$16.95**

**Spiritual Innovators:** Seventy-Five Extraordinary People Who Changed the World in the Past Century *Edited by Ira Rifkin and the Editors at SkyLight Paths; Foreword by Robert Coles*
6 x 9, 304 pp, b/w photographs, Quality PB, ISBN 1-893361-50-0 **$16.95**; HC, ISBN 1-893361-43-8 **$24.95**

**White Fire:** A Portrait of Women Spiritual Leaders in America
*by Rabbi Malka Drucker; Photographs by Gay Block*
7 x 10, 320 pp, 30+ b/w photos, HC, ISBN 1-893361-64-0 **$24.95**

# *Spirituality*

## Autumn: A Spiritual Biography of the Season
*Edited by Gary Schmidt and Susan M. Felch; Illustrations by Mary Azarian*
Autumn is a season of fruition and harvest, of thanksgiving and celebration of abundance and goodness of the earth. But it is also a season that starkly and realistically encourages us to see the limitations of our time. Warm and poignant pieces by Wendell Berry, David James Duncan, Robert Frost, A. Bartlett Giamatti, Kimiko Hahn, P. D. James, Julian of Norwich, Garret Keizer, Tracy Kidder, Anne Lamott, May Sarton, and many others rejoice in autumn as a time of preparation and reflection.
6 x 9, 320 pp, 5 b/w illus., Quality PB, ISBN 1-59473-118-7 **$18.99**; HC, ISBN 1-59473-005-9 **$22.99**

## Awakening the Spirit, Inspiring the Soul
### 30 Stories of Interspiritual Discovery in the Community of Faiths
*Edited by Brother Wayne Teasdale and Martha Howard, MD; Foreword by Joan Borysenko, PhD*
Thirty original spiritual mini-biographies that showcase the varied ways that people come to faith—and what that means—in today's multi-religious world.
6 x 9, 224 pp, HC, ISBN 1-59473-039-3 **$21.99**

## Winter: A Spiritual Biography of the Season
*Edited by Gary Schmidt and Susan M. Felch; Illustrations by Barry Moser*
Delves into the varied feelings that winter conjures in us, calling up both the barrenness and the beauty of the natural world in wintertime. Includes selections by Will Campbell, Rachel Carson, Annie Dillard, Donald Hall, Ron Hansen, Jane Kenyon, Jamaica Kincaid, Barry Lopez, Kathleen Norris, John Updike, E. B. White, and many others. "This outstanding anthology features top-flight nature and spirituality writers on the fierce, inexorable season of winter.... Remarkably lively and warm, despite the icy subject." —*Publishers Weekly* Starred Review
6 x 9, 288 pp, 6 b/w illus., Deluxe PB w/flaps, ISBN 1-893361-92-6 **$18.95**; HC, ISBN 1-893361-53-5 **$21.95**

**The Alphabet of Paradise:** An A–Z of Spirituality for Everyday Life
*by Howard Cooper* 5 x 7¼, 224 pp, Quality PB, ISBN 1-893361-80-2 **$16.95**

**Creating a Spiritual Retirement:** A Guide to the Unseen Possibilities in Our Lives
*by Molly Srode* 6 x 9, 208 pp, b/w photos, Quality PB, ISBN 1-59473-050-42 **$14.99**;
HC, ISBN 1-893361-75-6 **$19.95**

**The Geography of Faith:** Underground Conversations on Religious, Political and Social Change *by Daniel Berrigan and Robert Coles; Updated introduction and afterword by the authors* 6 x 9, 224 pp, Quality PB, ISBN 1-893361-40-3 **$16.95**

**God Lives in Glass:** Reflections of God for Adults through the Eyes of Children
*by Robert J. Landy, PhD; Foreword by Sandy Eisenberg Sasso*
7 x 6, 64 pp, HC, Full-color illus., ISBN 1-893361-30-6 **$12.95**

**God Within:** Our Spiritual Future—As Told by Today's New Adults   *Edited by Jon M.*
*Sweeney and the Editors at SkyLight Paths* 6 x 9, 176 pp, Quality PB, ISBN 1-893361-15-2 **$14.95**

**Jewish Spirituality:** A Brief Introduction for Christians   *by Lawrence Kushner*
5½ x 8½, 112 pp, Quality PB, ISBN 1-58023-150-0 **$12.95** *(a Jewish Lights book)*

## A Jewish Understanding of the New Testament
*by Rabbi Samuel Sandmel; New preface by Rabbi David Sandmel*
5½ x 8½, 384 pp, Quality PB, ISBN 1-59473-048-2 **$19.99**

**Journeys of Simplicity:** Traveling Light with Thomas Merton, Basho, Edward Abbey, Annie Dillard & Others   *by Philip Harnden* 5 x 7¼, 128 pp, HC, ISBN 1-893361-76-4 **$16.95**

**Keeping Spiritual Balance As We Grow Older:** More than 65 Creative Ways to Use Purpose, Prayer, and the Power of Spirit to Build a Meaningful Retirement
*by Molly and Bernie Srode* 8 x 8, 224 pp, Quality PB, ISBN 1-59473-042-3 **$16.99**

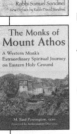

**The Monks of Mount Athos:** A Western Monk's Extraordinary Spiritual Journey on Eastern Holy Ground  *by M. Basil Pennington, ocso; Foreword by Archimandrite Dionysios*
6 x 9, 256 pp, 10+ b/w line drawings, Quality PB, ISBN 1-893361-78-0 **$18.95**

**One God Clapping:** The Spiritual Path of a Zen Rabbi   *by Alan Lew with Sherril Jaffe*
5½ x 8½, 336 pp, Quality PB, ISBN 1-58023-115-2 **$16.95** *(a Jewish Lights book)*

# Spirituality

**Prayer for People Who Think Too Much**
A Guide to Everyday, Anywhere Prayer from the World's Faith Traditions   by Mitch Finley
5½ x 8½, 224 pp, Quality PB, ISBN 1-893361-21-7  **$16.95**; HC, ISBN 1-893361-00-4  **$21.95**

**The Shaman's Quest:** Journeys in an Ancient Spiritual Practice
by Nevill Drury; with a Basic Introduction to Shamanism by Tom Cowan
5½ x 8½, 208 pp, Quality PB, ISBN 1-893361-68-3  **$16.95**

**Show Me Your Way:** The Complete Guide to Exploring Interfaith Spiritual Direction
by Howard A. Addison   5½ x 8½, 240 pp, Quality PB, ISBN 1-893361-41-1  **$16.95**;
HC, ISBN 1-893361-12-8 **$21.95**

**Spirituality 101:** The Indispensable Guide to Keeping—or Finding—Your Spiritual Life
on Campus   by Harriet L. Schwartz, with contributions from college students at nearly thirty campuses across the United States  6 x 9, 272 pp, Quality PB, ISBN 1-59473-000-8 **$16.99**

**Spiritually Incorrect:** Finding God in All the Wrong Places
by Dan Wakefield; Illus. by Marian DelVecchio
5½ x 8½, 192 pp, b/w illus., HC, ISBN 1-893361-88-8  **$21.95**

**Spiritual Manifestos:** Visions for Renewed Religious Life in America from Young
Spiritual Leaders of Many Faiths   Edited by Niles Elliot Goldstein; Preface by Martin E. Marty
6 x 9, 256 pp, HC, ISBN 1-893361-09-8  **$21.95**

**A Walk with Four Spiritual Guides:** Krishna, Buddha, Jesus, and Ramakrishna
by Andrew Harvey  5½ x 8½, 192 pp, 10 b/w photos & illus., HC, ISBN 1-893361-73-X  **$21.95**

**What Matters:** Spiritual Nourishment for Head and Heart
by Frederick Franck  5 x 7¼, 144 pp, 50+ b/w illus., HC, ISBN 1-59473-013-X  **$16.99**

**Who Is My God?, 2nd Edition**
An Innovative Guide to Finding Your Spiritual Identity
Created by the Editors at SkyLight Paths  6 x 9, 160 pp, Quality PB, ISBN 1-59473-014-8  **$15.99**

# Spirituality—A Week Inside

**Come and Sit:** A Week Inside Meditation Centers
by Marcia Z. Nelson; Foreword by Wayne Teasdale
The insider's guide to meditation in a variety of different spiritual traditions.
Traveling through Buddhist, Hindu, Christian, Jewish, and Sufi traditions, this essential guide takes you to different meditation centers to meet the teachers and students and learn about the practices, demystifying the meditation experience.
6 x 9, 224 pp, b/w photographs, Quality PB, ISBN 1-893361-35-7 **$16.95**

**Lighting the Lamp of Wisdom:** A Week Inside a Yoga Ashram
by John Ittner; Foreword by Dr. David Frawley
This insider's guide to Hindu spiritual life takes you into a typical week of retreat inside a yoga ashram to demystify the experience and show you what to expect from your own visit. Includes a discussion of worship services, meditation and yoga classes, chanting and music, work practice, and more.  6 x 9, 192 pp, b/w photographs, Quality PB, ISBN 1-893361-52-7 **$15.95**; HC, ISBN 1-893361-37-3  **$24.95**

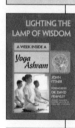

**Making a Heart for God:** A Week Inside a Catholic Monastery
by Dianne Aprile; Foreword by Brother Patrick Hart, ocso
This essential guide to experiencing life in a Catholic monastery takes you to the Abbey of Gethsemani—the Trappist monastery in Kentucky that was home to author Thomas Merton—to explore the details. "More balanced and informative than the popular *The Cloister Walk* by Kathleen Norris." —*Choice: Current Reviews for Academic Libraries*  6 x 9, 224 pp, b/w photographs, Quality PB, ISBN 1-893361-49-7 **$16.95**; HC, ISBN 1-893361-14-4 **$21.95**

**Waking Up:** A Week Inside a Zen Monastery
by Jack Maguire; Foreword by John Daido Loori, Roshi
An essential guide to what it's like to spend a week inside a Zen Buddhist monastery.
6 x 9, 224 pp, b/w photographs, Quality PB, ISBN 1-893361-55-1  **$16.95**;
HC, ISBN 1-893361-13-6  **$21.95**

# Spiritual Practice

### Divining the Body
Reclaim the Holiness of Your Physical Self   *by Jan Phillips*
A practical and inspiring guidebook for connecting the body and soul in spiritual practice. Leads you into a milieu of reverence, mystery, and delight, helping you discover a redeemed sense of self.
8 x 8, 256 pp, Quality PB, ISBN 1-59473-080-6 **$16.99**

### Finding Time for the Timeless
Spirituality in the Workweek   *by John McQuiston II*
Simple, refreshing stories that provide you with examples of how you can refocus and enrich your daily life using prayer or meditation, ritual, and other forms of spiritual practice.   5½ x 6¼, 208 pp, HC, ISBN 1-59473-035-0 **$17.99**

### The Gospel of Thomas: A Guidebook for Spiritual Practice
*by Ron Miller; Translations by Stevan Davies*
An innovative guide to bring a new spiritual classic into daily life. Offers a way to translate the wisdom of the Gospel of Thomas into daily practice, manifesting in your life the same consciousness revealed in Jesus of Nazareth. Written for readers of all religious backgrounds, this guidebook will help you to apply Jesus's wisdom to your own life and to the world around you.
6 x 9, 160 pp, Quality PB, ISBN 1-59473-047-4 **$14.99**

### The Knitting Way: A Guide to Spiritual Self-Discovery
*by Linda Skolnik and Janice MacDaniels*
Through sharing stories, hands-on explorations, and daily cultivation, Skolnik and MacDaniels help you see beyond the surface of a simple craft in order to discover ways in which nuances of knitting can apply to the larger scheme of life and spirituality. Includes original knitting patterns.
7 x 9, 240 pp, Quality PB, ISBN 1-59473-079-2 **$16.99**

**Earth, Water, Fire, and Air:** Essential Ways of Connecting to Spirit
*by Cait Johnson   6 x 9, 224 pp, HC, ISBN 1-893361-65-9* **$19.95**

### Forty Days to Begin a Spiritual Life
Today's Most Inspiring Teachers Help You on Your Way
*Edited by Maura Shaw and the Editors at SkyLight Paths; Foreword by Dan Wakefield*
7 x 9, 144 pp, Quality PB, ISBN 1-893361-48-9 **$16.95**

### Labyrinths from the Outside In
Walking to Spiritual Insight—A Beginner's Guide
*by Donna Schaper and Carole Ann Camp*
6 x 9, 208 pp, b/w illus. and photographs, Quality PB, ISBN 1-893361-18-7 **$16.95**

**Practicing the Sacred Art of Listening:** A Guide to Enrich Your Relationships and Kindle Your Spiritual Life—The Listening Center Workshop
*by Kay Lindahl   8 x 8, 176 pp, Quality PB, ISBN 1-893361-85-3* **$16.95**

**The Sacred Art of Bowing:** Preparing to Practice
*by Andi Young   5½ x 8½, 128 pp, b/w illus., Quality PB, ISBN 1-893361-82-9* **$14.95**

**The Sacred Art of Chant:** Preparing to Practice
*by Ana Hernandez   5½ x 8½, 192 pp, Quality PB, ISBN 1-59473-036-9* **$15.99**

**The Sacred Art of Fasting:** Preparing to Practice
*by Thomas Ryan, CSP   5½ x 8½, 192 pp, Quality PB, ISBN 1-59473-078-4* **$15.99**

**The Sacred Art of Listening:** Forty Reflections for Cultivating a Spiritual Practice
*by Kay Lindahl; Illustrations by Amy Schnapper*
8 x 8, 160 pp, Illus., Quality PB, ISBN 1-893361-44-6 **$16.99**

**Sacred Speech:** A Practical Guide for Keeping Spirit in Your Speech
*by Rev. Donna Schaper   6 x 9, 176 pp, Quality PB, ISBN 1-59473-068-7* **$15.99**;
*HC, ISBN 1-893361-74-8* **$21.95**

# Spiritual Poetry—The Mystic Poets

Experience these mystic poets as you never have before. Each beautiful, compact book includes: A brief introduction to the poet's time and place; a summary of the major themes of the poet's mysticism and religious tradition; essential selections from the poet's most important works; and an appreciative preface by a contemporary spiritual writer.

## Hafiz: The Mystic Poets
*Preface by Ibrahim Gamard*
Hafiz is known throughout the world as Persia's greatest poet, with sales of his poems in Iran today only surpassed by those of the Qur'an itself. His probing and joyful verse speaks to people from all backgrounds who long to taste and feel divine love and experience harmony with all living things.
5 x 7¼, 144 pp, HC, ISBN 1-59473-009-1 **$16.99**

## Hopkins: The Mystic Poets
*Preface by Rev. Thomas Ryan, CSP*
Gerard Manley Hopkins, Christian mystical poet, is beloved for his use of fresh language and startling metaphors to describe the world around him. Although his verse is lovely, beneath the surface lies a searching soul, wrestling with and yearning for God.
5 x 7¼, 112 pp, HC, ISBN 1-59473-010-5 **$16.99**

## Tagore: The Mystic Poets
*Preface by Swami Adiswarananda*
Rabindranath Tagore is often considered the "Shakespeare" of modern India. A great mystic, Tagore was the teacher of W. B. Yeats and Robert Frost, the close friend of Albert Einstein and Mahatma Gandhi, and the winner of the Nobel Prize for Literature. This beautiful sampling of Tagore's two most important works, *The Gardener* and *Gitanjali,* offers a glimpse into his spiritual vision that has inspired people around the world.
5 x 7¼, 144 pp, HC, ISBN 1-59473-008-3 **$16.99**

## Whitman: The Mystic Poets
*Preface by Gary David Comstock*
Walt Whitman was the most innovative and influential poet of the nineteenth century. This beautiful sampling of Whitman's most important poetry from *Leaves of Grass,* and selections from his prose writings, offers a glimpse into the spiritual side of his most radical themes—love for country, love for others, and love of Self.
5 x 7¼, 192 pp, HC, ISBN 1-59473-041-5 **$16.99**

# Sacred Texts—SkyLight Illuminations Series

## Andrew Harvey, series editor

Offers today's spiritual seeker an enjoyable entry into the great classic texts of the world's spiritual traditions. Each classic is presented in an accessible translation, with facing pages of guided commentary from experts, giving you the keys you need to understand the history, context, and meaning of the text. This series enables readers of all backgrounds to experience and understand classic spiritual texts directly, and to make them a part of their lives. Andrew Harvey writes the foreword to each volume, an insightful, personal introduction to each classic.

### Bhagavad Gita: Annotated & Explained
*Translation by Shri Purohit Swami; Annotation by Kendra Crossen Burroughs*
"The very best Gita for first-time readers." —Ken Wilber. Millions of people turn daily to India's most beloved holy book, whose universal appeal has made it popular with non-Hindus and Hindus alike. This edition introduces you to the characters, explains references and philosophical terms, shares the interpretations of famous spiritual leaders and scholars, and more.
5½ x 8½, 192 pp, Quality PB, ISBN 1-893361-28-4 **$16.95**

### Dhammapada: Annotated & Explained
*Translation by Max Müller and revised by Jack Maguire; Annotation by Jack Maguire*
The Dhammapada—believed to have been spoken by the Buddha himself over 2,500 years ago—contain most of Buddhism's central teachings. This timeless text concisely and inspirationally portrays the route a person travels as he or she advances toward enlightenment and describes the fundamental role of mental conditioning in making us who we are.
5½ x 8½, 160 pp, b/w photographs, Quality PB, ISBN 1-893361-42-X **$14.95**

### The Divine Feminine in Biblical Wisdom Literature
Selections Annotated & Explained
*Translation and annotation by Rabbi Rami Shapiro; Foreword by Rev. Dr. Cynthia Bourgeault*
Uses the Hebrew books of Psalms, Proverbs, Song of Songs, Ecclesiastes and Job, and the Wisdom literature books of Sirach and the Wisdom of Solomon to clarify who Wisdom is, what She teaches, and how Her words can help us live justly, wisely, and with compassion.
5½ x 8½, 240 pp, Quality PB, ISBN 1-59473-109-8 **$16.99**

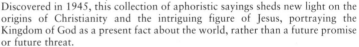

### The Gospel of Thomas: Annotated & Explained
*Translation and annotation by Stevan Davies*
Discovered in 1945, this collection of aphoristic sayings sheds new light on the origins of Christianity and the intriguing figure of Jesus, portraying the Kingdom of God as a present fact about the world, rather than a future promise or future threat.
5½ x 8½, 192 pp, Quality PB, ISBN 1-893361-45-4 **$16.95**

### Hasidic Tales: Annotated & Explained
*Translation and annotation by Rabbi Rami Shapiro*
Introduces the legendary tales of the impassioned Hasidic rabbis, which demonstrate the spiritual power of unabashed joy, offer lessons for leading a holy life, and remind us that the Divine can be found in the everyday.
5½ x 8½, 240 pp, Quality PB, ISBN 1-893361-86-1 **$16.95**

### The Hebrew Prophets: Selections Annotated & Explained
*Translation and annotation by Rabbi Rami Shapiro*
Focuses on the central themes covered by all the Hebrew prophets: moving from ignorance to wisdom, injustice to justice, cruelty to compassion, and despair to joy, and challenges us to engage in justice, kindness, and humility in every aspect of our lives.
5½ x 8½, 224 pp, Quality PB, ISBN 1-59473-037-7 **$16.99**

# Sacred Texts—SkyLight Illuminations Series
## Andrew Harvey, series editor

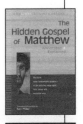

### The Hidden Gospel of Matthew: Annotated & Explained
*Translation and annotation by Ron Miller*
Takes you deep into the text cherished around the world to discover the words and events that have the strongest connection to the historical Jesus. Reveals the underlying story of Matthew, a story that transcends the traditional theme of an atoning death and focuses instead on Jesus's radical call for personal transformation and social change.
5½ x 8½, 272 pp, Quality PB, ISBN 1-59473-038-5 **$16.99**

### The Secret Book of John
#### The Gnostic Gospel—Annotated & Explained
*Translation and annotation by Stevan Davies*
Introduces the most significant and influential text of the ancient Gnostic religion. This central myth of Gnosticism tells the story of how God fell from perfect Oneness to imprisonment in the material world, and how by knowing our divine nature and our divine origins—that we are one with God—we reverse God's descent and find our salvation.
5½ x 8½, 208 pp, Quality PB, ISBN 1-59473-082-2 **$16.99**

### Rumi and Islam: Selections from His Stories, Poems, and Discourses—Annotated & Explained
*Translation and annotation by Ibrahim Gamard*
Offers a new way of thinking about Rumi's poetry. Focuses on Rumi's place within the Sufi tradition of Islam, providing insight into the mystical side of the religion—one that has love of God at its core and sublime wisdom teachings as its pathways.
5½ x 8½, 240 pp, Quality PB, ISBN 1-59473-002-4 **$15.99**

### Selections from the Gospel of Sri Ramakrishna
#### Annotated & Explained
*Translation by Swami Nikhilananda; Annotation by Kendra Crossen Burroughs*
The words of India's greatest example of God-consciousness and mystical ecstasy in recent history. Introduces the fascinating world of the Indian mystic and the universal appeal of his message that has inspired millions of devotees for more than a century.
5½ x 8½, 240 pp, b/w photographs, Quality PB, ISBN 1-893361-46-2 **$16.95**

### The Way of a Pilgrim: Annotated & Explained
*Translation and annotation by Gleb Pokrovsky*
This classic of Russian spirituality is the delightful account of one man who sets out to learn the prayer of the heart—also known as the "Jesus prayer"—and how the practice transforms his life.
5½ x 8½, 160 pp, Illus., Quality PB, ISBN 1-893361-31-4 **$14.95**

### Zohar: Annotated & Explained
*Translation and annotation by Daniel C. Matt*
The best-selling author of *The Essential Kabbalah* brings together in one place the most important teachings of the Zohar, the canonical text of Jewish mystical tradition. Guides you step by step through the midrash, mystical fantasy, and Hebrew scripture that make up the Zohar, explaining the inner meanings in facing-page commentary.
5½ x 8½, 176 pp, Quality PB, ISBN 1-893361-51-9 **$15.99**

# About SKYLIGHT PATHS Publishing

SkyLight Paths Publishing is creating a place where people of different spiritual traditions come together for challenge and inspiration, a place where we can help each other understand the mystery that lies at the heart of our existence.

Through spirituality, our religious beliefs are increasingly becoming a part of our lives—rather than *apart* from our lives. While many of us may be more interested than ever in spiritual growth, we may be less firmly planted in traditional religion. Yet, we do want to deepen our relationship to the sacred, to learn from our own as well as from other faith traditions, and to practice in new ways.

SkyLight Paths sees both believers and seekers as a community that increasingly transcends traditional boundaries of religion and denomination—people wanting to learn from each other, *walking together, finding the way.*

For your information and convenience, at the back of this book we have provided a list of other SkyLight Paths books you might find interesting and useful. They cover the following subjects:

| | | |
|---|---|---|
| Buddhism / Zen | Gnosticism | Mysticism |
| Catholicism | Hinduism / | Poetry |
| Children's Books | Vedanta | Prayer |
| Christianity | Inspiration | Religious Etiquette |
| Comparative | Islam / Sufism | Retirement |
| Religion | Judaism / Kabbalah / | Spiritual Biography |
| Current Events | Enneagram | Spiritual Direction |
| Earth-Based | Meditation | Spirituality |
| Spirituality | Midrash Fiction | Women's Interest |
| Global Spiritual | Monasticism | Worship |
| Perspectives | | |

*Or phone, fax, mail or e-mail to:* SKYLIGHT PATHS Publishing
Sunset Farm Offices, Route 4 • P.O. Box 237 • Woodstock, Vermont 05091
Tel: (802) 457-4000 • Fax: (802) 457-4004 • www.skylightpaths.com
**Credit card orders:** (800) 962-4544 (8:30AM–5:30PM ET Monday–Friday)
Generous discounts on quantity orders. SATISFACTION GUARANTEED. Prices subject to change.